BIRDS

112 BIRDS IN FULL COLOR

A GUIDE TO THE MOST FAMILIAR AMERICAN BIRDS

by

HERBERT S. ZIM, Ph.D.

Educational Consultant, U. S. Fish and Wildlife Service

and

IRA N. GABRIELSON, LL.D., D.Sc.

President, Wildlife Management Institute
Former Director, U. S. Fish and Wildlife Service

ILLUSTRATED BY JAMES GORDON IRVING

Sponsored by The Wildlife Management Institute

A GOLDEN NATURE GUIDE

SIMON AND SCHUSTER · NEW YORK

FOREWORD

This book pictures in full color 112 of the most familiar American birds. Using these birds as keys, the book mentions additional related and similar species, helping the reader to identify over 260 birds in all.

The selection for this book of the most common birds of America and the assembling of concise information about them were achieved through long, detailed study of voluminous data on our bird life. This might have been an impossible task were it not for the wholehearted cooperation and assistance of ornithologists and others on the professional staff of the U.S. Fish and Wildlife Service. Dr. Clarence A. Cottam, Mr. A. L. Nelson, Dr. A. C. Martin, Dr. John Aldrich, and Mr. Robert E. Stewart gave helpful comments and suggestions. Special thanks are due to Chandler S. Robbins, biologist of the Patuxent Research Refuge, who compiled the basic data for the range maps and who checked migration dates, tabular data, and other factual information. Gordon Irving has contributed his knowledge of birds as well as his unusual artistic talent.

Thanks are due also to Charles E. O'Brien, Assistant Curator, and Alexander Seidel, of the Department of Birds, American Museum of Natural History.

Published by Simon and Schuster, Inc., Rockefeller Center, New York 20.

HOW TO USE THIS BOOK

This is a field book made to fit your pocket when you go looking for birds. Check each range map (example below) to see if the bird occurs in your region. Concentrate on these birds. Areas where birds live in summer are shown in red on the maps; winter areas are in blue. Purple shows areas where the bird is a permanent resident. Migrating birds pass over parts of the white areas of the maps in spring and fall. Check their "time table" on pages 128 to 149, where you will also find information on nests, eggs, and food. Mark each bird you are likely to see, and when you have seen it enter the place and date on the "Record" pages. Thumb through this book and become familiar with the birds. Then, when you see them, you'll recognize some at first sight.

The more you look at this book, the more facts you'll find. The color plates show spring plumage of male birds, and sometimes females and young. The text emphasizes field markings; size; important facts; related birds which are similar in appearance; and differences between males and females. The birds have been selected so that knowing one bird will help you to know others like it.

The 112 birds illustrated were selected after a careful study of all American birds. They are among the most common and the ones you have the best chance of seeing. No rare birds or birds of limited range are included. In almost every part of this country you can see many of the birds pictured and described in this book — plus other common local birds you will soon learn to know.

SEEING BIRDS

You have been seeing birds as far back as you can remember and you will continue seeing them wherever you may be. It's a real pleasure to see them. You can see more birds and more kinds of birds by learning how to look. This book will help you. It is not written for the expert, but for people who want to see birds just for the joy of it.

Begin by giving your attention to the birds in your own vicinity. These are the birds to learn first. Don't try to memorize the details of size, shape, or color of head, wing, or tail. Learn to know the whole bird as one total picture, since one glance at a moving bird may be all you'll get. When you can recognize a flicker or an Oven-bird, then concentrate on the markings that make it stand out: color, habits, the way it moves, its special kind of flight, and—most important—its song and calls. Each of these will help you to know the bird you see.

You will find more people interested in birds than you might imagine. Sometimes they're organized in clubs. Some just get together and go looking for birds. They will be at camps, at the seashore, and in most out-of-door places. They will share whatever they know with you. If you are beginning, remember that everyone was once a beginner. If you want to identify birds, ask questions and then ask more. Before you know it, people will be coming to you with their questions.

Practice is essential. Go looking for birds as often as you can. As to time of day, early mornings are best. By the time the sun is well up, bird activity slows down and does not resume till late afternoon. Marsh birds are most active near dawn or in the evening, but ducks, waterfowl, and hawks may be seen all day. Make bird watching a week-end habit the year round. Try getting out early on spring mornings when the birds are migrating north. Follow and observe them as they nest in the summer. Watch them as they form flocks and start south in the fall. You learn something from every bird you see.

EQUIPMENT. The only essential equipment for seeing birds is a pair of eyes. Good ears are a help, too. But there are ways of increasing your enjoyment, none of which involves much expense. This book is one, for a guide book is important. As you acquire experience, you will want more advanced books (see page 150). In this book is space to keep records. Your own records, if kept systematically, are an important part of your equipment. A pocket notebook to record more detailed information is worth carrying. Old clothing, waterproof shoes, and a bottle of mosquito repellent are part of an experienced bird watcher's equipment.

Field glasses or binoculars are the most important and most expensive item of equipment. There's no denying their value in bringing tree-top birds down to you. Like a good camera, a good pair of glasses is a precision tool and should be selected with care. The best glasses are made with prisms to reduce their size. The power of the glass tells how much closer it makes a bird appear. Through 3 x (power) glasses a bird looks three times as close. Glasses of 3 x to 8 x are best. Remember, the higher the power, the more limited your field of vision. Glasses that admit the most light are the best. This depends on the width of the front lens (usually measured in millimeters). A 6 x 30 lens admits more light than a 6 x 24. Glasses that adjust by a single center focusing screw are much more convenient. Don't be in a hurry to buy glasses.

Ask other bird watchers first; learn something of costs. A good pair of glasses is a lifetime investment. Plan for them, even if you must do without for a while.

WHERE TO LOOK. Birds are everywhere, but to see the most birds try looking in the best places: in moist woodlands or perhaps at the edge of a wooded swamp. Young scrubby woods are likely to have more birds than mature forests. Wood margins are generally a good place to visit, especially during migration. But no single place is best. Salt-water marshes and shores will yield birds that one will never find in pine woods. Many species prefer open fields, others the dry Western deserts. You may have no other choice than a city park, but a wooded area in the midst of a city is one of the very best places to look for birds during the migration periods. If you explore your own region, you will discover certain spots are favored—perhaps a small glen with a brook, or a wooded point extending into a lake; a marsh, a spring, or cottonwoods along a river. A varied countryside is likely to be richer in variety of birds than an unchanging landscape.

HOW TO LOOK. Dashing through the woods will get you nothing but shortness of breath. Experienced watchers will often sit quietly in a likely spot and let the birds come to them. Keen-eyed birds are easily frightened by movement. Don't make yourself conspicuous against the open sky. Move slowly; and the less time spent on the move, the better. Try to cover several distinct areas, if possible— a woodland, marsh, field, river bank, shore, or whatever your locality affords. Eventually you will work out a route which will give you the greatest returns in birds seen for the time spent. Experience in your own region will be your best help.

WHY LOOK? When a person is really interested, there's nothing like the thrill of seeing a beautiful bird, identifying a species you have never seen before, and watching your records grow. All of our extensive knowledge about birds has come from bird watching. We have learned something of the importance of birds in the world of wild life and know how they help control the many insects that plague us. Your own garden may not be much better off, but—by and large—birds help hold insects in check. We have discovered that a single kind of bird is neither "good" nor "bad," but that all birds from hawks to hummingbirds have their important natural place. Some birds do occasional damage; some birds are occasionally a direct help to man; but these are both exceptions and are not typical of the total picture of bird life.

From watching birds we discover more about their food and habits and so are able to do more to protect those that need help in order to survive. Perhaps you may be able to help in establishing a local bird "refuge"—an area where passing birds can rest and feed and where resident birds can nest. Once you have made a start in seeing birds, you may want to do more than just look. The section on Amateur Activities (page 16) suggests some things for you to do.

PARTS OF A BIRD

Names are tools. Bird experts have dozens of scientific names for the various parts of birds. Using these scientifically defined terms, they can describe a bird with great accuracy. The beginner does not have the experience to use these terms even if he knew them. So only a minimum of technical terms is used in this book. When you see a bird you cannot identify and want help from some expert, try to observe the bird so well that you can describe its size, habits, and the color and form of the parts illustrated above. Put your information down on paper (don't trust your memory). By keeping these few parts in mind you will systematize your observations and secure the details needed to get your bird identified.

BIRD CLASSIFICATION

Scientists have placed related birds into groups (orders, families, and genera) if their bills, feet, and form of wing are similar. If you know these groups, the relationship and classification of birds will be clearer. These groups also call attention to body parts that are not important in field identification, but are essential in the scientific study of birds. Here is a simplified list of the main bird groups found in this book:

LOONS: Large swimming and diving birds; tails short; legs set far back. Four toes: 3 front ones fully webbed. Bill sharply pointed, higher than wide.

GREBES: Smaller swimmers and divers. Tail lacking; legs far back. Four toes with thin skin flaps (lobes) and with flattened nails. Bill slender, pointed; higher than wide.

HERONS and BITTERNS: Long-legged wading birds. In flight, feet extend beyond tail but neck is pulled in. Bill straight and sharp; skin between eye and bill bare. Four toes, scarcely webbed or not webbed at all. Middle toenail has comb-like margin.

DUCKS, GEESE, and SWANS: Swimming birds with distinct tails. Legs centered. Birds walk well compared to grebes and loons. Four toes: front 3 webbed. Bill broad and flat, often with "teeth" along edge. Upper bill ending in short, flat hook or "nail."

HAWKS, EAGLES, and VULTURES: Large birds. Bill strongly hooked; feet powerful, claws long and curved. Vultures differ in having a bare head with nostrils connected by hole through bill.

GROUSE, QUAIL, and TURKEY: Land birds which scratch for food. Bills short and stout. Feet heavy, strong; hind toe short and raised. Wings short and rounded, with stiff feathers.

CRANES, RAILS, and COOTS: Marsh birds flying with neck extended and feet dangling (rails); wings rounded. Four toes, unwebbed (except for Coot, which has lobes). Middle toenail without comb-like margin (see Herons). Patch between eye and bill is feathered.

PLOVERS, SANDPIPERS, and SNIPES: Long-legged shore birds, mostly small. Bill usually conical, long and soft; nostrils opening through slits in bill. Generally 4 toes: hind toe raised and short. Sanderlings and most plovers have only 3 toes.

GULLS and TERNS: Mostly light-colored marine birds. Wings long, narrow and pointed. Bill hooked (gulls) or pointed (terns) with nostrils opening into slits that go through bill. Four toes: hind toe small and not webbed.

PIGEONS and DOVES: Small-headed birds with slender bills, grooved at base; and with nostrils opening through a bare fleshy area at base of bill. Legs short. Four toes: all on same level. Hind toe as long as shortest front one.

CUCKOOS: Long, slim birds with slightly curved bill. Tail long, feathers not stiff or pointed; central tail feathers longest. Four toes: 2 in front; 2 behind.

OWLS: Bills strongly hooked. A swelling at its base is concealed by feathers. Toes with large curved claws; entire leg feathered. Eyes large and immovable in puffy, feathered "face."

NIGHTHAWKS: Birds with large heads, small bills and wide mouths. Bill usually with bristles at base. Feet small; middle toe long with comb-like claw. Feathers soft, dull-colored.

SWIFTS: Small swallowlike birds; bill small with no bristles at base. Mouth wide. Wings slender and very long, reaching beyond tail; tail with 10 feathers.

HUMMINGBIRDS: Tiny birds with bill slender and needle-like—longer than head. Feet small, weak. Feathers on back usually shiny green.

KINGFISHERS: Head large and crested. Bill long, strong, pointed. Feet small and weak. Four toes: 2 of the 3 forward toes joined for half their length.

WOODPECKERS: Climbing birds. Bill strong, pointed, with bristles at nostril. Tail feathers stiff and pointed. Four toes: 2 in front, 2 in back; or (rarely) 3: 2 in front and 1 in back.

PERCHING BIRDS: The largest bird group. Land birds, mostly small, with 4 toes—all on the same level, never webbed. Hind toe as long as middle front toe—an adaptation for perching. Tail with 12 feathers.

AMATEUR ACTIVITIES

Everyone starts watching birds with the same ideas in mind: to learn their names, to identify as many as possible, and to see what kind of "records" his watching will yield. Some people are very happy doing these things and never go beyond this stage. Others find many more things to do. Time, place, and experience will determine what you want to do. Here are some suggestions:

ATTRACTING BIRDS BY FEEDING. Birds were here long before people fed them—and they will continue to feed and care for themselves. But if severe storms completely cut off the food supply of winter birds, large-scale cooperative efforts are sometimes essential to save them. It's another story if you want to attract birds to a particular place during winter—as your own yard or window. Then feeding will help. Feeding means more than scattering scraps of bread around. Find out the best way to build feeding stations. Set them near shrubbery to give birds shelter. Place lumps of suet in wire containers for creepers, chickadees, nuthatches, and woodpeckers. Small grain (sunflower seeds, hemp, millet, and canary seed) will attract seed eaters. At a window station you can observe the birds as they feed.

ATTRACTING BIRDS BY WATERING. Birds need drinking and bathing water just as much as they need food. A watering place will attract more birds during warm months when wild food is available. Birds like moving, shallow water. A trickle of water running into a one-inch pan with gravel on the bottom is excellent. Nothing elaborate is needed. An old bucket with a drip hole hung over an old baking pan will do as well as any elaborately constructed cement pool.

ATTRACTING BIRDS WITH COVER AND SHELTER.

Birds need cover for protection against wind, cold, and enemies. The best kind of cover for birds is shrubs and vines that provide food as well as a place to hide. Plants that look attractive to us are not necessarily attractive to birds. Native plants that retain their fruit in winter are best. Nesting boxes are seldom satisfactory unless they are built with a specific bird in mind. A box for a wren must be very different from one for a flicker. Get complete instructions and follow them. Build a box that can be easily cleaned and used year after year. Don't place boxes too closely; three or four nesting boxes to an acre are usually enough. Most birds set up their own "territory" and will keep other birds out.

CREATING A LOCAL REFUGE.

A group of people may find a way to create a local bird refuge to help birds care for themselves. Not all places are suitable, but most communities have swamp or wasteland which can easily be developed into a bird refuge. Parks, golf courses, and cemeteries have been successful. Ample water supply is needed. Small dams across a brook will create shallow ponds that attract many birds. Swamp plants and grasses should be encouraged as seed producers. Evergreens may be planted for shelter.

BIRD PHOTOGRAPHY. Hunting with a gun is giving way to hunting with a camera. Only a few species of game birds may be shot, but you can photograph any bird you can approach. Bird photography offers thrills and plenty of hard work. Don't begin until you really understand photography. A flash bulb is usually necessary even in daylight, because many birds prefer deep woodland shade. A fast lens is essential, too. Bird photography calls for patience, skill, and real effort, but one fine shot makes it all worth while.

BIRD BANDING. Sooner or later every bird watcher learns about the thin aluminum bands put around birds' legs as an essential part of the scientific field study of birds. Now nearly six million birds have been banded. From them we have learned much about migrations, routes, life span, movements of young, population changes, and the return of individuals to the same locality annually.

You can aid this research, for the cooperation of thousands of amateurs has made the scientific study of birds possible. If you find a banded sick or dead bird, except a pigeon, look for a serial number, like "41-345678" or "A-669785," and for an address that may read, "F. & W. Serv. Wash. D.C." Write the number on a postcard, stating when, where, how, and by whom the bird was found. Send the card to the Bird-Banding Office, Patuxent Research Refuge, Laurel, Maryland. In reply you will receive the history of the bird you found. And the information you gave will have helped to complete one more record.

Permits to band birds are issued to qualified persons by the U. S. Fish and Wildlife Service. An applicant must be at least 18 years old, and three experts must vouch for his ability to identify birds. He must be willing to accept the responsibilities that go with scientific work. The official aluminum bands and record forms are supplied free.

BIRD COUNTS AND CENSUSES. As soon as you can recognize the common birds, you will begin to keep lists of species you see. This is the beginning of what may become an important hobby. As you get to know birds better, your lists will include estimates of the number of birds seen as well as the kinds of birds. The next step is to concentrate on a specific area and do a complete census. The resulting figures may give an idea of the density of the bird population there. Many bird clubs make such a count on Christmas day, and this gives a spot check on the winter bird population all over the country. Counts made during the breeding season help determine the number of adult birds per acre. This varies from 2 to 20 birds with type of land and the locality. Carefully made counts, especially those repeated year after year on one tract of land, are of real scientific value. Special counts made during migrations, counts of bird colonies or bird roosts, help us understand more about certain unusual species.

LIFE HISTORIES. So much is still unknown about the way birds live that any careful observer can gather new information of scientific value. The ability to make immediate detailed records of what you see is essential, and you must continue watching and recording till the story is complete. We have so much more to learn about songs, flight patterns, courtship, nesting, feeding habits, care and training of young, behavior of males and females, etc., that there is work for all bird watchers who care to join in. During a summer vacation a well-prepared amateur can add definitely to our knowledge of some bird by observing even a few nesting pairs and recording complete data about them. Preparations for this work should include reading some of the excellent life histories of birds that have already been written.

THE BIRDS AT A GLANCE. The data on individual birds on pages 21-126 are supplemented by tables on pages 128-148. These give in concise form, for the same birds and in the same order, a wealth of facts on migrations, areas of summer and winter residence, eggs, nests, and foods.

The information on bird migrations is given by key cities: DC—Washington, D.C.; NY—New York; B—Boston; StL—St. Louis; SF—San Francisco; P—Portland, Ore. It is usually pertinent for a radius of 100 miles. You can estimate the arrival of birds in your region from data given for the key cities: There is about a week's difference between DC and NY and between NY and B for most migrating birds.

Birds found in an area the year round are listed as "permanent residents." Others come North in spring, stay all summer, and depart in the fall. For these "summer residents" (SR), the table gives the average date of arrival and departure. Such birds may be seen at any time between the two dates—and sometimes a bit earlier or later. Other birds come in the fall, stay all winter, and move North again in spring. Average dates for these "winter residents" (WR), are similarly given. Finally, some birds come North in the spring and, after staying a while, continue northward. These can be seen only for a few weeks in spring and on their way South in the fall. These birds are "transients" (Tr). Approximate dates for all birds are given in abbreviated form: E, M, and L stand for "early," "middle," and "late." "E-Apr" means early April and "M-Oct" stands for middle October.

Always remember that local weather and other factors influence arrival and departure of birds. After several years, your own personal records may prove a better local guide.

LOON. Spot loons by their large size, long body, short neck, pointed bill, and loud, yodel-like call. Loons are expert divers, but kick along the water before taking off in flight. In winter they are gray above and white beneath. Red-throated Loon (25 in.) is a smaller species with reddish throat. Pacific Loon (24 in.) is similar to the Red-throated, but with a black throat. —*Length: 28-36 in. Female similar to male.*

PIED-BILLED GREBE. Grebes are expert divers and swimmers. Smaller than most ducks, they float lower in the water. The Pied-billed is darker in winter, when throat and bill markings are lacking. It has a more rounded bill than other grebes. The Horned Grebe is the same size; head black with chestnut "ear patches." Holboell Grebe (19 in.) is grayer, with white cheeks and a pointed, yellowish bill.—*Length: 12-15 in. Female similar to male.*

GREAT BLUE HERON. This largest common wader flies with a slow, regular wing beat. It nests in colonies, but often nests alone. Call: a low-pitched croak. Distinct from any other bird, because of its size. American Egret (38 in.), almost as large and all white, has yellow bill and black legs and feet. Snowy Egret, definitely smaller (24 in.), is similar, with black bill and legs, yellow feet.—*Length: 42-50 in. Female and young similar to male.*

GREEN HERON. This common heron lives and nests alone. A dark bird, scarcely larger than a crow, it has a typical heron flight. May be confused with the Bittern or Night Heron at a distance, but its yellow-orange legs are distinctive. Raises crest when alarmed. Adult Little

Blue Heron (25 in.) is more slender and dark all over; young are white with dull wing tips, yellow-green legs and feet; may be confused with the Egrets.—*Length: 15-22 in. Female and young similar to male.*

BLACK-CROWNED NIGHT HERON. An old tree crowned with these roosting herons is a memorable sight. These colonial birds feed their young night and day. They are the only heron completely white below and dark above. Young are spotted and may be confused with Bitterns. The low-pitched, hoarse "quock" is often heard at night. Yellow-crowned Night Heron, a more southern species, is similar, with black head, white crown, and short white stripe on cheek. — *Length: 22-28 in. Female similar to male.*

BITTERN. The American Bittern rarely ventures outside marshes. It does not perch in the open like other herons. It hides among reeds and cattails and "freezes" when in danger. In flight, its black wing tips distinguish it from young Night Herons. The Bittern's "pumping" song is

unique. The Least Bittern, much smaller (12 in.), has a dark back, buff on the wings and below; more often heard than seen; call soft like the Cuckoo's.—*Length: 23-24 in. Female and young similar to male.*

CANADA GOOSE. Recognized by its size, long black neck, and white cheeks, this is a very well-known and very widely distributed waterfowl. Geese swim with their necks straight up and fly, in striking V-formation, with necks outstretched. They feed in ponds but also graze on grass and sprouting grain. The five sub-species differ in size and range from the small Cackling Goose (24 in.) to the large Common Canada Goose.— *Length: 35-40 in. Female similar but smaller than male.*

MALLARD. This large, common marshland duck has a blue wing patch margined by two white bars. These marks identify it in any plumage. The green head and white neck ring are good field marks of the male. Mallards take off in a vertical leap and fly fast. They feed, like all surface ducks, by tipping in shallow water. Mallards have been domesticated and have crossed with other ducks. — *Length: 19¼-28 in. Female smaller than male, mottled brown and buff.*

BLACK DUCK. This most common eastern duck resembles the female Mallard, but is darker and lacks white on wings and tail. Males have bright-red legs and yellowish bills. Black Ducks, like Mallards, prefer fresh or brackish water. The Mottled or Dusky Duck (20 in.) is much like the Black, but restricted to Florida and Gulf Coast. The western Gadwall (20 in.) differs from Black Duck in its smaller size, white belly, and small, rectangular white wing patch.—*Length: 22-26 in. Female smaller but similar to male.*

WOOD DUCK. The male lacks brilliant colors during the summer, when it resembles the duller female, although its bill is always brighter. Recognize it in flight by its short neck, white trailing edge to wing, and bill held at a distinct downward angle. Wood Ducks fly low, dodging around trees, in which they roost. Distinguished from Baldpate (20 in.) in flight by lack of large, white patch on forward edge of wings.—*Length: 17-20 in. Female smaller than male, duller, with white eye ring.*

PINTAIL. Spot the Pintail by its long, pointed tail, slender neck, and in flight by the white stripe on trailing edge of its wing. This most common western duck practically leaps into the air when taking off. It is a surface feeder, preferring fresh water with Mallards and Black Ducks. It rarely dives. The female lacks the long pointed tail. It is similar to the female Mallard and Black Duck, but without the blue patch on wing.— *Length: 26-30 in. Female smaller; lacks solid brown head.*

CANVAS-BACK. This duck swims low in water and dives rapidly. A long bill and low, sloping forehead are distinguishing marks. In flight, note its large size, white body, and the wings far back on the body. Redhead (20 in.) similar at a distance, but smaller and with darker back and abrupt forehead.—*Length: 20-24 in. Female with olive head and neck.*

MERGANSER. Loonlike birds with narrow, cylindrical "toothed" bill, Mergansers fly low, prefer open water; dive when frightened. In flight, note the white on wings. The American Merganser is largest—conspicuously white with a small crest. The Red-breasted Merganser (22 in.), rufous breast and larger crest, prefers salt water. The smaller Hooded Merganser (18 in.) has a fan-shaped white crest.—*Length: 21-27 in. Female smaller, gray with reddish head and feet, sharply defined white throat.*

COOT. A ducklike bird, living in marshes and along rivers. Coots are the only ducklike birds with a chalky white bill. Coots are close relatives of the gallinules, which are slightly smaller in size. Both swim with a pumping motion of the neck. The Coot's white bill contrasts with the Florida Gallinule's red one. Coots dive rapidly but, when frightened, skit over the water with feet and wings.—*Length: 13-16 in. Female very similar to male.*

KILLDEER. A large plover marked by a double breast band and (in flight) by its orange-brown rump and tail. It frequents open meadows and plowed fields, where its loud "killdeer" call often resounds. The Killdeer bobs its head as it walks. The young leave the nest almost as soon as hatched. The Semipalmated Plover (7 in.) is similar in color to the Killdeer, but with only one breast band. It prefers mudflats and beaches. — *Length: 9-11 in. Female nearly identical with male.*

WILSON SNIPE. This shy bird of meadows and open fresh-water swamps rises high in the spring air and circles with an unforgettable "drumming" sound; otherwise it keeps well concealed. Field marks are pointed wings, very long bill, rather short legs, and zigzag flight. The plump Woodcock of woodlands and dry fields, a close

 relative, has rounded wings and a richer brown color. The Dowitcher (11 in.), of mudflats and beaches, has white rump and in spring is reddish beneath. *Length: 10¼-11¾ in. Female similar to male, larger.*

GREATER YELLOW-LEGS. This gray-and-white sandpiper is one of the largest and most conspicuous of our shore birds. In flight, note its size, the white rump and tail. Its black, slightly upturned bill and long, bright yellow legs are the best field marks. The Lesser Yellow-legs (10 in.) is very similar, with a shorter bill. Willets (16 in.) are larger birds, with dark legs and conspicuous black-and-white wing markings in flight.— *Length: 13-15 in. Female larger, but similar to male.*

SPOTTED SANDPIPER. The Spotted Sandpiper is the only one with a strongly spotted breast—but the spots are present in the breeding plumage only. In many inland localities it is the most common shore bird, and the only fresh-water sandpiper. It typically teeters up and down as it walks. The Solitary Sandpiper (8 in.) is similar, but with a white eye ring and white on sides of tail. Both these sandpipers have dark legs. — *Length: 7½-9 in. Female practically identical with male.*

LEAST SANDPIPER. Best known and smallest of the small sandpipers, this is a bird of mudflats and salt marshes. Note its small size, chocolate-brown back, greenish legs, and slender, straight bill. The Semipalmated Sandpiper (6 in.), found with the Least, has a grayer back, stouter bill, and black legs. The Western Sandpiper (6½ in.) has a longer, heavier bill. The White-rumped Sandpiper (7½ in.) is larger, with a distinct white rump.—*Length: 5-6½ in. Female very similar to male.*

HERRING GULL. This bird, abundant along the Atlantic coast and parts of the interior, is a great scavenger. Immature birds are dull gray-brown, becoming lighter with maturity. Adults have gray wings and back, black wing tips, and flesh-colored legs. The Ring-billed Gull, similar but smaller (19 in.), has dull yellow legs and a black ring on its bill. Laughing Gull (17 in.) in the east and Franklin Gull in west have black head and darker back. California Gull resembles Herring Gull.— *Length: 22½-26 in.*

COMMON TERN. Terns are smaller than gulls, more graceful, with forked tails and slender wings. They plummet headlong into the sea after fish. Common Tern is distinguished by its colorful bill, dusky wing tips, and deeply forked, white tail. Arctic Tern (15 in.) is slightly grayer, with redder bill and shorter legs. Forster Tern—lighter bill, lighter wing tips, and grayer tail— and Roseate Tern (both 15 in.)—slender black bill and more deeply forked tail—are both like the Common Tern.—*Length: 13-16 in. Female similar; young with darker bills.*

COOPER HAWK. This is typically a bird of the woods, rarely soaring in the open. Its short, rounded wings and long, rounded tail make it easy to identify in flight. It's an aggressive, often destructive, species. The Sharp-shinned Hawk is similar, but smaller (12 in.), with a

square-tipped tail and lighter crown. Goshawk, larger than Cooper (23 in.), has light gray breast, dark gray back, and white line over eye.— *Length: 14-18 in. Female larger; young with streaked breast.*

RED-TAILED HAWK. The Red-tailed is a large, soaring hawk. Its wings are broad but its tail, fan-shaped and chestnut-red above, is not always visible. This hawk is light underneath with dark streaks across the belly. Red-shouldered Hawk is similar with a distinctly banded tail. Other soaring hawks include the small Broad-winged Hawk (16 in.) of the East with its prominently barred tail; and Swainson Hawk (21 in.) of the West with its broad, dark breast band.—*Length: 19-22 in. Female larger, but similar. Young with dark, faintly barred tail.*

TURKEY & BLACK VULTURES. Vultures—valuable scavengers—are protected by law. They soar motionless in wide circles. Turkey Vultures hold their long wings slightly above the horizontal line. The naked red head completes identification of adult Turkey Vultures. The smaller Black Vulture is a more southern species with round, white patches on the underside of its wing tips. It has a dark head (as do the young Turkey Vultures) and a very short, square tail.—*Length: Turkey—26-32 in. Black—24-27 in. Females same as males.*

Turkey

Both

SPARROW HAWK. This is the smallest falcon—a hawk with long, pointed wings. Note the rich reddish-brown on its back, tail, and crown. The female's tail has narrow black bars. The Pigeon Hawk, slightly larger (12½ in.), lacks the reddish patches and has heavy black bars on the tail. The Duck Hawk, a less common but wide-ranging species (17 in.), has black mustache marks. Duck Hawks are trained for hunting birds and rabbits.—*Length: 8¾-10¾ in. Female slightly larger.*

BALD EAGLE. Eagles are large, long-winged hawks. They soar with their wings horizontal (vultures, with their wings slightly raised). The white head and tail mark the adult Bald Eagle. Younger birds are dark-brown all over. Eagles are frequently found near water, as fish is their

favorite food. The Golden Eagle (30-43 in.) of the West is dark, except for the white base of its tail and white near the wing tips.—*Length: 30-34 in. Female larger, otherwise similar.*

OSPREY. The Osprey or Fish Hawk resembles the Eagle, but is distinctly smaller and slimmer with much white beneath. It flies with a decided backward bend at the "elbow" of the wing. The huge nest of the Osprey is similar to the Bald Eagle's. A group of nests is a sight to remember. The birds wheel and soar over the sea, plunging feet foremost after fish.— *Length: 21-24½ in. Female and young similar to male.*

RING-NECKED PHEASANT. This unmistakable Asiatic bird was successfully introduced in the West and is now found over much of the United States. It is a favorite game bird of farmlands, where it garnishes waste grain, occasionally causing local crop damage. The handsome male is unrivaled in its splendid coloring. The female is smaller,

dull brown, with a shorter but also pointed tail, which distinguishes it from Ruffed Grouse and Prairie Chickens.—*Length: 33-36 in. Female smaller, duller brown and white.*

RUFFED GROUSE. This is the only large, chickenlike bird of the deep woods. It suddenly springs into the air with a whirring beat of wings. The drumming of the male is part of the spring courting. The fan-shaped tail with its broad, black terminal band is the best field mark. The Prairie Chicken (18 in.) of the midwest is somewhat similar but with a dark, rounded tail; it prefers open country. Several other grouse are found in the West and North.—*Length: 15½-19 in. Female smaller, duller.*

BOB-WHITE. Everyone knows the Bob-white by its call, but these small quail, so well camouflaged in dead grass and weeds, are hard to see. Their size, ruddy color, and stubby appearance make Bob-whites easy to identify once they are spotted. Hunters prize the bird as game. Western quail (Valley, Gambel, Plumed and Mearns) are about the same size as the Bob-white, but differ in appearance. All these have some kind of plume on their heads.—*Length: 9½-10¾ in. Female larger, duller.*

PIGEON. Pigeons, variable in color, are descendants of the wild Rock Dove of Europe. Though handsome birds, their nesting habits make them undesirable in cities. The Common Pigeon has a broad, fanlike tail. The large western Band-tailed Pigeon (15½ in.) has yellow legs and a white band on top of the tail. The White-crowned Pigeon of Florida is a dark pigeon with a whitish crown. The tiny Ground Dove (6¾ in.) of the extreme South has a short black tail and rufous flight feathers.—*Length: 11-13 in. Sexes similar.*

MOURNING DOVE. Slimmer than the pigeon and with a long, pointed tail, the Mourning Dove nests in every state. It is named from its melancholy call: "Coo-ah, coo, coo, coo." The white tail border is conspicuous in flight. The White-winged Dove (12 in.) of the West is somewhat similar in appearance, but has a large white wing stripe.

The southwestern Inca Dove (8 in.) resembles a miniature Mourning Dove. Doves are seed and fruit eaters and are prized as game birds. — *Length: 11-13 in. Female duller, with a shorter tail.*

SCREECH OWL. The only small owl with eartufts, this owl is found in two color phases: a gray and a reddish brown. Like most owls, this is a bird of the night, when its descending wailing call is heard. The real "Screech Owl" is a European bird. Keen eyesight and noiseless flight enable our Screech Owl to prey on field rodents. The Burrowing Owl (9 in.) of the West and the northern Saw-whet Owl (8 in.) lack the distinct eartufts of the Screech Owl.— *Length: 8-10 in. Adults and young similar.*

BARN OWL. The long-legged Barn Owl is unique. Its white, heart-shaped face and dark eyes are unmistakable. In flight the light buff plumage is conspicuous. Color varies from bird to bird, some being quite dark. The

Barn Owl, which nests in barns, belfries, and hollow trees, is important in controlling rodents injurious to orchard and garden crops. It has no close relatives. — *Length: 15-21 in. Adults and young similar.*

HORNED OWL. This aggressive, powerful bird resembles an overgrown gray Screech Owl. Its call is a deep, penetrating hoot, repeated five to seven times. In flight it looks like a large-headed neckless hawk. The smaller Long-eared Owl (15 in.) has similar eartufts. The eastern Barred Owl (20 in.) and the western Spotted Owl (19 in.) have dark eyes and lack eartufts. The Barred Owl gives eight hoots; the Spotted, three or four.— *Length: 18-25 in. Female much larger.*

YELLOW-BILLED CUCKOO. This slim, brown-and-white cuckoo is dovelike in appearance. It rarely lays eggs in the nests of other birds like the European cuckoo. Cuckoos are among the few birds that eat hairy caterpillars. The Yellow-billed Cuckoo has a yellowish under-bill, chestnut-

brown on wings, and conspicuous white tail spots. The Black-billed Cuckoo, similar in size, lacks the yellow bill and chestnut wings; its tail spots are indistinct.—*Length: 11-12½ in. Adults and young similar.*

CHIMNEY SWIFT. These birds are almost always in the air, flying with a batlike flight. Their short, spiny tails prop them against the inside walls of chimneys when resting. Distinctive, streamlined birds, swifts usually fly in groups and migrate in large flocks. There are three western swifts: Vaux Swift (4½ in.) similar to the Chimney; Black (7¼ in.) and White-throated (7 in.) Swifts— both larger and each colored as its name implies,—*Length: 4¾-5½ in. Adults and young similar.*

WHIP-POOR-WILL. Resting on dead leaves, the Whip-poor-will is practically invisible—more often heard than seen. It does not fly much, except when feeding. Its rounded tail (tipped white in the male) and absence of white in the wing distinguish it from the Nighthawk. The Chuck-will's-widow (12½ in.) of the South is larger, with buff on the throat and under the tail. Poor-will, a western species, is smaller (7½ in.) and grayer.—*Length: 9-10¼ in. Female smaller.*

NIGHTHAWK. A close relative of the Whip-poor-will, the Nighthawk is darker and has a longer, slightly forked tail. In the air, note its distinguishing white wing spot. Nighthawks are constantly in the air, flying in a zig-zag path, circling, diving, and banking as they feed on flying insects. The Texas Nighthawk (8½ in.) of the southwest is very similar, with white band nearer tip of wing. It is a low-flying bird.—*Length: 8¼- 10 in. Female smaller, lighter, and without white band on tail.*

RUBY-THROATED HUMMINGBIRD. These eastern hummingbirds are gems of beauty and marvels in flight. They hover motionless, can fly backward, and may be attracted to brightly-colored tubes of sugar water hung in gardens. Western hummingbirds include the very similar Broad-tailed (4½ in.) of the Rockies; the Anna (4 in.), crown and throat of metallic red; the Black-chinned (3¾- in.), black chin and purple throat band; and the brown-backed Rufous Hummingbird (3½ in.).—*Length: 3-3¾ in. Female and young white-throated.*

Others

Ruby-throated

BELTED KINGFISHER. Where there are fish there are kingfishers, beating the air in irregular flight, diving into water with a splash and emerging with fish in their beaks. Note the ragged crest, heavy black bill, and harsh, rattling call. The tiny Texas Kingfisher (7 in.) of southern Texas has a dark green back. — *Length: 11-14 in. Male same size, without chestnut sides and breast.*

RED-HEADED WOODPECKER. The only eastern wood-pecker with a completely red head. The solid black back and large, white wing patches are good field marks. The California Woodpecker (9½ in.) has a black back, black chin, and black breast band. The Red-bellied Wood-pecker (10 in.) of the southeast has horizontal black and white barring across the back; back of neck and entire crown are red. Woodpeckers can cling to vertical trunks, propped by stiff tail feathers.—*Length: 8½-9¾ in. Adults similar.*

Red-headed

California

FLICKER. A large, distinctly brown woodpecker. Its bobbing flight, white rump, golden wing linings, and black breast band aid identification. Often found on the ground hunting for ants. Like all woodpeckers, it nests in a cavity of a dead trunk or branch. The western Red-shafted Flicker (13 in.) has red under the wings and a red mustache mark. The two flickers have crossed. Hybrids are common in the midwest.—*Length: 12-13 in. Female and young similar, but adult female lacks black "mustache" at base of bill.*

Western or Red-shafted

Eastern or Yellow-shafted

YELLOW-BELLIED SAPSUCKER. The sapsucker feeds on the soft inner bark and sap of trees. Note the vertical white patch on the black wing. The Pacific Red-breasted Sapsucker, a subspecies of the Yellow-bellied, is similar, but with head and breast solid red. The Red-naped Sapsucker of the Rockies also has a red head, but with a black border and a black breast patch. In the northwest, Williamson Sapsucker is slightly larger, mostly black, with a white rump and large white wing patch.—*Length: 7¾-8¾ in. Female smaller, lacks red on throat.*

DOWNY WOODPECKER. The Downy and the Hairy Woodpecker are both common and nearly identical except for size. The Hairy is larger by some 2 in. and has a much heavier black bill. Both males have a small red head patch, lacking in the females. The vertical, white stripe down the back is a field mark worth noting for both. The Downy feeds with chickadees and nuthatches in winter, and often visits feeding stations. — Length: 6¼-7¼ in. Female smaller; lacks red on head. Young like adults.

KINGBIRD. From its perch on a branch or fence this bird darts after insects in true flycatcher fashion. The white tip of the tail marks eastern species. The Gray Kingbird (9 in.) of the southeast lacks this, is paler, with an oversized bill. The western or "Arkansas" Kingbird

(9 in.) is gray, with yellow belly and black tail edged white on the sides. The similar Cassin Kingbird of the western mountains has whiter throat, no white on tail.—*Length: 8½-9 in. Young and adults alike.*

CRESTED FLYCATCHER. This large flycatcher is the only eastern one with a reddish tail. The yellow belly and wing bars should be noted as good field marks. The Crested Flycatcher is an orchard and forest bird which typically uses shed snake skins in its nest. It may be confused with the Western Kingbird, except for the reddish tail. The similar Ash-throated Flycatcher (8 in.) replaces the Crested Flycatcher in the West.— *Length: 8-9¼ in. Young and adults similar.*

Ash-throated

Crested

PHOEBE. If the persistent "phoebe" call doesn't identify this bird, its equally persistent tail-bobbing will. The Eastern Phoebe is an inconspicuous gray flycatcher, with no good field marks. It returns to the same nesting site year after year. The Say Phoebe (7½ in.) is a western bird with rusty breast and belly. The Wood Pewee (6 in.) looks like a phoebe with two distinct wing bars; it does not bob its tail.—*Length: 6¼-7¼ in. Adults similar. Young with dull wing bars.*

Say

Eastern

LEAST FLYCATCHER. On this smallest flycatcher note the two whitish wing bars and eye ring. It is most difficult to tell this flycatcher from three similar eastern species—the Alder, Acadian, and Yellow-bellied. The latter has a decided yellowish tint. The Acadian is the only one found in the southeast. It is equally hard to identify, in the West, the Hammond, Wright, Traill, and Western Flycatchers. It seems best to forget details and call all small flycatchers "Empidonax"—the Latin name for the whole group.— *Length: 5-5¾ in. Young and adults similar.*

HORNED LARK. Flocks of Horned Larks feed in bare fields and along shores, walking as they feed. Note black collar, yellowish throat, black tail, and, at close range, the "horns." This and European Skylark are true larks. The Meadowlark is a Blackbird. The Pipit (6½ in.), unrelated to the Horned Lark, is sometimes taken for it. The Pipit also walks; head brownish, faintly streaked; outer tail feathers white.— *Length: 6¾-8 in. Female duller, young streaked.*

PURPLE MARTIN. The Martins are the largest and most conspicuous of the swallows. The adult male is a uniform violet. The female and young males have a grayish breast. In flight their wings are more triangular than other swallows'. Martins nest in colonies and make use of martin houses. The Rough-winged Swallow (5½ in.), which nests singly, often in holes in gravel banks, is similar, with a plain brown back and no violet.—*Length: 7¼-8½ in. Female has grayish breast and white belly.*

TREE SWALLOW. Unbroken blue-black above and unbroken white below makes the Tree Swallow a striking bird, especially when large flocks gather to migrate in the fall. Young birds are brown-backed, but have entirely white underparts. This swallow varies its insect diet with

bayberries for which it has a persistent appetite. The western Violetgreen Swallow (5½ in.) is similar with a white patch on each side of its rump.—*Length: 5-6¼ in. Female duller.*

BARN SWALLOW. This is the one swallow with a *deeply* forked "swallow tail." Note the chestnut forehead and throat, and the buff undersides. The only other swallow with similar color is the Cliff Swallow (5½ in.), with short, squared tail, buff rump, and white forehead. The Bank Swallow (5 in.) is a brown-backed bird with a brown band across its white breast. All swallows are usually found near water.—*Length: 5¾-7¾ in. Female duller and with shorter tail.*

MAGPIE. No other bird resembles the large black-and-white Magpie with its sweeping tail. There are two species, distinguished chiefly by their bills. The American Magpie has a black, the other a yellow, bill. The Yellow-billed Magpie (17 in.) is found in the valleys of central California. Magpies fly and feed in flocks. Their mixed diet includes fruits, melons, and other crop plants. They often live around ranches, and occasionally these relatives of the Crow become serious local pests.—*Length: 17½-21 in. Females similar to male.*

American

Yellow-billed

CROW. People often confuse two related birds with the all-too-familiar common Crow. The coastal Fish Crow (17 in.) is similar except for its short nasal call: "car, car." The large Raven (24 in.), rare in the East, has rough throat feathers and a distinct croaking call. It soars in flight, showing clearly its wedge-shaped tail.—*Length: 17-21 in. Female somewhat smaller.*

BLUE JAY. No other eastern bird is like the noisy Blue Jay, with its striking blue, black, and white color. Of the western jays, the Steller (13 in.) has a black head, throat, and breast, and long black crest. The short-tailed, crestless, Piñon Jay (11 in.) is dull blue with a darker crown.

The Scrub or "California" Jay (12 in.), found west of the Rockies and in Florida, has a blue cap, back, wings, and tail, and a dull blue necklace across the whitish underparts. — *Length: 11-12½ in. Young similar.*

WHITE-BREASTED NUTHATCH. Nuthatches creep down tree trunks head first. The White-breasted Nuthatch (white sides of head, throat, and breast) is the common eastern bird. The smaller Red-breasted Nuthatch (4½ in.) has dark line through the eye, and orange-brown underparts. The Brown-headed Nuthatch (4½ in.), of southeast pine woods, has a chocolate cap. The Pygmy Nuthatch (4½ in.) of the West has a dull gray cap, enclosing the eyes. Nuthatches often feed at feeding stations.—*Length: 5-6¼ in. Female and young duller.*

BLACK-CAPPED CHICKADEE. This plump chickadee needs no introduction. Its call is its name. The Chickadee, a constant visitor to feeding stations, often feeds upside down. The smaller (4½ in.) Carolina Chickadee—south of the Mason and Dixon line—has four or five notes in its whistled song instead of two or three. The Brown-capped Chickadee (5 in.) is a winter visitor along the eastern Canadian border. The western Chestnut-backed Chickadee has a dull brown cap and a bright chestnut back.—*Length: 4¾-5¾ in. Female and young similar.*

TUFTED TITMOUSE. There is nothing outstanding about this pert, gray woodland bird except its crest. No other small gray bird has this ornament. It's distinguished from the Chickadee by its lack of a bib and from the Nuthatch by its stubby bill and perching habit. The chestnut flanks are a confirming mark. The Plain Titmouse (5½ in.) of the West lacks this, but is otherwise similar. The tiny western Bush-tit (4 in.) is a nondescript gray-brown bird with a long tail, a dull brown cap, but no crest.—*Length: 5½-6½ in. Young and adults similar.*

BROWN CREEPER. This is the only small, brown tree-creeping bird. Its undersides are white, its tail stiff. It always works up the tree in a spiral, searching for insects and grubs, which it digs out with its curved bill. Then it flies to base of next tree and creeps up again. The male

and female look alike and both blend with bark and so are difficult to detect. Creepers prefer open, mature woodlands. They feed in small flocks in the company of woodpeckers, chickadees, and kinglets. — *Length: 5-5¾ in. Young and adults similar.*

HOUSE WREN. Wrens are small, pert, brown birds which usually carry their tails almost vertical. The House Wren is best known. It is a brownish bird which lacks distinct head markings. The Winter Wren (4 in.) has a darker belly, shorter tail, and light line over the eye. The long-tailed Bewick Wren (5¼ in.) also has a white eye stripe, and its tail is faintly bordered with white. The Carolina Wren (6 in.) has a large white eye stripe and a ruddy back. The western Wrens include the Cañon Wren (5½ in.) with a white throat and dark belly, and the Rock Wren (6 in.) with very faint breast streaks and buff-fringed tail. — *Length: 4¼-5¼ in. Young and adults similar.*

MOCKINGBIRD. "Listen to the Mockingbird . . ." goes the song, and the Mockingbird is, indeed, worth hearing. Its song imitates other birds' songs, with something original added. Mockingbirds nest around homes. In the West, they are even common in the streets. They are slender,

gray, with white outer tail feathers and white wing patches. The Shrike (9 in.) is a chunkier bird with a thicker bill and a black mask through the eyes.—*Length: 9-11 in. Young and adults similar.*

CATBIRD. Not quite as attractive looking as the Mockingbird, the Catbird sings almost as well. Its name comes from its mewing call. Catbirds prefer shrubs and vines near houses. They are slaty-gray, except for a black cap and a chestnut patch at the underside base of the tail. No other birds are quite like them, though some female blackbirds are grayish. Catbirds usually raise two broods a season. The male aids considerably in their care.—*Length: 8¼-9¼ in. Young and adults similar.*

BROWN THRASHER. One of eight related birds, these thrashers have long tails and curved bills. They feed and nest near the ground. The handsome Brown Thrasher is a rich chestnut above and streaked with brown below. The California Thrasher (12 in.) is dark brown and unstreaked; no wing bars. The Le Conte Thrasher (11 in.)

is an ashy-gray-backed desert bird with a plain, whitish breast. In the far West, the heavily streaked Sage Thrasher (8½ in.) has white tips on its outer tailfeathers.—*Length: 10¼-12 in. Female similar to male.*

ROBIN. This bird's average length (10 in.) is a standard to which other birds are compared. It is the most common native bird of the East and also the largest of the thrushes—a relationship seen in the spotted breasts of the young. Two or three broods are raised each year. Homesick colonists named the Robin after a European bird with a much redder breast. The Varied Thrush of the Pacific coast states is similar to the Robin, but has a dark breast band.—*Length: 9-10¾ in. Female similar but duller, breast paler.*

WOOD THRUSH. These thrushes are typically woodland birds, recognized by their chestnut-brown backs, redder heads, heavily spotted breasts, and clear, flutelike song. The Hermit Thrush (7 in.) and the Veery (7 in.) also have bright red-brown backs. The Veery has a uniformly colored back and only a few faint spots on its

breast. The longer-tailed Brown Thrasher may be confused with the Wood Thrush, but its breast is streaked instead of spotted and its eye is yellow.—*Length: 7½-8½ in. Young and adults similar.*

HERMIT THRUSH. Famous songster, the Hermit Thrush reverses the Wood Thrush pattern. Its *tail*, which it slowly raises and lowers, is redder than its back. The breast is less spotted than the Wood Thrush's, but more than the Veery's. Other thrushes have dull, olive-brown backs. The Olive-backed Thrush (7 in.) has a buff eye ring and buff cheeks. The Gray-cheeked Thrush (7 in.), an Eastern migrant, has gray cheek patches and no eye ring.—*Length: 6½-7½ in.* Young and adults similar.

BLUEBIRD. The Bluebird is welcomed as the first migrant of spring. It is a thrush also, as the faintly spotted breast of the young testifies. Though other birds are blue, none has the chestnut brown breast of this species. The Western Bluebird has a chestnut patch on the back as well. The adult male Mountain Bluebird of the Rockies has a blue back, pale blue breast, and white belly. Bluebirds are often attracted to the correct type of nesting box.— *Length: 6¼-7¾ in. Female and young much duller.*

BLUE-GRAY GNATCATCHER. With its long, white-bordered tail, the Gnatcatcher looks like a miniature Mockingbird. It is seldom seen, because of its preference for tree tops in moist woods. The blue back and white eye ring aid identification; so does the bird's habit of jerking its tail. The Plumbeous Gnatcatcher (4½ in.) is a western desert species with a black cap, less white on the tail, and a generally duller color than the Blue-gray Gnatcatcher.—Length: 4-5 in. Female grayer, tinged with brown.

RUBY-CROWNED KINGLET. This kinglet is plainer than the Golden-crowned. Its red crown is often hidden, except when the male is angry. Its large white eye ring and wing bars distinguish this kinglet when its ruby crown does not show. Both kinglets are nervous in flight and when feeding. In summer, kinglets breed in Northern spruce forests. In winter they are often found in company with Brown Creepers, nuthatches, chickadees, and Downy

Woodpeckers. Kinglets are frequently seen in shrubbery about buildings, sometimes using window and outdoor feeding stations.—*Length: 3¾-4¼ in. Female lacks red crown.*

GOLDEN-CROWNED KINGLET. The kinglets are among our smallest birds and are doubly attractive because they are usually winter visitors. Their small, chunky bodies, stubby tails, and dull, olive-gray color are distinctive. The Golden-crowned Kinglet is the more showy of the two American species. The female has a golden crown bordered with black and white. The male has an orange stripe through the center of the golden crown. These kinglets are commonly seen feeding on the branches of firs, spruce, and other conifers.—*Length: 3-4¼ in. Female with yellow crown.*

CEDAR WAXWING. These warm-brown, crested birds cannot be mistaken, especially when a flock is feeding on cherries or mulberries. Watch for the wide yellow band that tips the tail. The grayer Bohemian Waxwing (8 in.) of the northwest has a bright cinnamon patch underneath, at the base of its tail. Bohemian Waxwings occasionally

appear in the north central states. Their irregular and unpredictable appearances make these waxwings birds of mystery.—*Length: 6½-8 in. Female similar to male. Young streaked below.*

LOGGERHEAD SHRIKE. Shrikes feed on insects, rodents, and even small birds. They often hang their prey on thorns or barbed-wire fences. Resembling mockingbirds slightly, the shrikes are heavier, have a black eye mask and a hooked bill. Their peculiar bounding flight is worth noting. The Northern Shrike is a larger species (10 in.) and has a faintly barred breast; its black mask is divided by the bill, which is light on the underside. It is seen only during winter months.— *Length: 9-9½ in. Female similar to male. Young browner.*

STARLING. Introduced into New York in 1890, Starlings have been spreading ever since. In some places they are a nuisance and even a pest. But Starlings are handsome birds, given to musical song and mimicry. Sunlight on their plumage makes a rainbow of colors. Note the short tail,

plump body, and (in spring and summer) yellow bill. Younger birds are uniform brown with dark bills, and adults (in winter) are speckled with white.—*Length: 7½-8½ in. Female similar to male.*

Yellow Warbler

WARBLERS

There are 109 species of American warblers. Fifty-six of these occur in the United States and include some of our most beautiful birds. Over twice as many warblers are found in the East as in the West. Next to the sparrows, they are the largest family of American birds and to many people the most exciting to watch. Most warblers winter in the tropics. As they migrate North, many rest and feed high in the trees and so are not easily seen, though an experienced watcher may see as many as 25 kinds of warblers on a warm May day if he searches enough. The warblers' songs may be hard for the novice to distinguish, but once known, they help considerably in finding and identifying these birds.

Warblers are small, characterized by their straight, slender bills. Their food is mainly insects, which they catch on trees or on the wing. In spring the bright colors of the males are striking. Females are usually not as brightly colored. In fall, when warblers move south, they are harder to recognize in their dull, autumn plumage. The only one likely to be seen in winter in the East north of Florida is the Myrtle Warbler. It winters in bayberry bushes on the coast, as far north as Massachusetts.

YELLOW WARBLER. The Yellow Warbler is the only warbler that is practically all yellow and has yellow spots on the tail. Closer observation reveals the chestnut-streaked breast. The Yellow Warbler prefers shrubs or

low trees and so is easily seen. The female Hooded Warbler of the southeast is similar to the Yellow, but has white tail spots.—*Length: 4¾-5¼ in. Female and young lack breast spots.*

BLACK AND WHITE WARBLER. Only two eastern warblers are striped black and white: the common Black and White and the Black-poll (5 in.), which has a solid black crown and is seen only during migration. The Black

and White Warbler stays close to tree trunks and heavy branches. The Western Black-throated Gray Warbler is somewhat similar.— *Length: 5-5½ in. Female and young lack black throat.*

BLACK-THROATED BLUE WARBLER. Here is a really descriptive bird name. The blue-gray back, black face and throat, and white belly clearly mark this trim warbler. No other warbler has this bold color pattern. The Black-

throated Blue is typically a bird of the open woodlands. The Black-throated Green Warbler (5 in.) of the East has a yellow-green back and golden face.—*Length: 4¾-5½ in. Female olive-brown with small white spot on wing.*

YELLOW-THROAT. This is a warbler of marshes and wayside shrubbery. The black mask and yellow throat mark the male. The female has the yellow throat without the mask. Its whitish belly and absence of wing bars help

identification. The Kentucky Warbler (5½ in.) of the southeastern woodlands has a large yellow eye ring, more black on the head, the underparts entirely yellow.—*Length: 4½-5¾ in. Female duller without black mask.*

OVEN-BIRD. Another ground-loving warbler often seen walking on the ground, its tail bobbing. The Oven-bird is somewhat like a small thrush in appearance: olive-brown above with a striped breast. The orange crown with black

borders and a distinct eye ring make identification positive. Its often-repeated "teacher" song is as easy to learn as any.—*Length: 5½-6½ in. Female like male. Young lack orange crown.*

WATER-THRUSH. These plump warblers stay close to the ground in swamps and along brooks. The Northern Water-thrush has a distinct yellowish cast to the under parts and a yellowish eye line. The more southern Louisi-

ana Water-thrush is white where the Northern is yellow. It lacks the streaked throat. Both species teeter like miniature sandpipers.—*Length: 5-6¼ in. Female and young similar.*

MYRTLE WARBLER. The yellow rump, crown, and sides mark the Myrtle Warbler. The Myrtle migrates early in spring and later in the fall than any other common eastern warbler. The yellow-rumped Magnolia Warbler (5 in.) of the East has a black-streaked yellow breast and

much white in tail and wings. Audubon Warbler (5 in.) of the West is very similar to the Myrtle, but with a yellow instead of a white throat.— *Length: 5-6 in. Female and young browner; less yellow on crown and sides.*

REDSTART. The male, black, with red wing- and tail-patches, is a striking bird. The female is duller, with yellow instead of the red and with white underparts. The pattern is unmistakable. Redstarts continually flit about,

flycatcher fashion, feeding on insects.—*Length: 4½-5¾ in. Female smaller, duller, with yellow wing and tail patches.*

WILSON WARBLER. A small, very active warbler, unbroken yellow below, duller above. The male has a black cap which is lacking in the female. The female is a nondescript yellow bird with no other markings. This species,

which prefers moist grounds and swamps, is much commoner in the West (where it is called the Pileolated Warbler) than in the East.— *Length: 5-5¾ in. Female lacks black cap.*

RED-EYED VIREO. Vireos are a bit larger and less active than warblers. The Red-eyed has a gray crown bordered with black, a broad white line above the eye, and no wing bars. The Warbling Vireo has a paler eye line. Note the pale yellow eye ring and two wing bars of the White-eyed Vireo (5 in.). The Yellow-throated (6 in.) of the East and the Blue-headed (6 in.) Vireos are like the White-eyed, but differ as their names indicate.—*Length: 5½-6½ in. Female identical; young with brown eye.*

HOUSE SPARROW. This bird, misnamed English Sparrow, is not particularly a native of England and definitely is not a sparrow. It is a relative of the weaver finches. Imported from England in 1850, it became established, spread rapidly, and is now a serious pest. The House Sparrow may be easily confused with our native sparrows. The gray crown and black throat of the male are characteristic, as are the unstreaked crown and broad buff line over the eye of the female. —Length: 5½-6½ in. Female duller and lacks black.

BOBOLINK. The male, entirely black below, is easy to identify. But the female and the male in winter are very sparrowlike in appearance, with buff breasts and black and buff stripes on the crown. In the South, the Bobolink, known as the Reedbird, may do serious damage to the

rice crop. The other grains it eats are of negligible value. The melodic song aids identification when the birds are hidden in tall marsh grasses.—*Length: 6¼-8 in. Female and male in fall are sparrow-like.*

MEADOWLARK. As more land was farmed, Meadowlarks thrived, for they are birds of meadows and grain fields. The only other large birds with white outer tail feathers are the mockingbird and shrike. Watch for the black V on the Meadowlark's yellow breast. The Western Meadowlark (9 in.) is slightly paler, with more yellow on the sides of its throat. Its song is louder and more musical than the simple whistle of the eastern bird.—*Length: 9-11 in. Female smaller, darker, and duller.*

BREWER BLACKBIRD. This is the Blackbird of western ranches and corrals. The yellowish eye of the male and the purplish tinge to its black feathers are field marks. The Brewer Blackbird walks with its wings slightly drooped. The female is brownish-gray with brown eyes. The Rusty Blackbird (9 in.) of the East is a similar pale-eyed bird, but with a distinct rusty tinge. The female is gray with a blue and green sheen.— *Length: 7¾-9¾ in. Female smaller, browner, with dark eyes.*

RED-WING. No other bird resembles the male Red-wing —its red shoulder patches with buff margins are unmistakable. The female, lacking this distinctive mark, is a dusky brown with a heavily streaked breast. The Tricolored Red-wing (8 in.) of the Pacific coast has even deeper red shoulders with a white margin. All Red-wings are marsh birds. They gather in large flocks during fall, winter, and spring.—*Length: 9-10 in. Female brown; no shoulder patches.*

BALTIMORE ORIOLE. The brilliant male is a showy bird. The female is a dull orange-yellow with two pale wing bars. Bullock Oriole (8 in.) of the West is like the Baltimore but has orange on sides of head and over eye. The Orchard Oriole (6½ in.) of the East is also similar, but

with chestnut instead of orange. The female Orchard Oriole is similar to the female Baltimore but is greenish-yellow instead of orange-yellow.— *Length: 7-8¼ in. Female and young dull orange-yellow, with wing bars.*

GRACKLE. Grackles are large blackbirds with long, wedge-shaped tails. The Purple Grackle and the Bronzed Grackle are most common. They are distinguished by the color of their backs—either purple with iridescent barring, or plain bronze. They often cross. Intermediate birds are seen south of New York. The Boat-tailed Grackle (16 in.) of the South is found along the coast except in Florida, where it is found inland also. —*Length: 9½-12 in. Female smaller and duller.*

COWBIRD. This bird has the unusual habit of laying one or more eggs in nests of other birds. The eggs hatch in ten days—sooner than most other birds'. With this start the fast-growing Cowbirds monopolize the nest. The Cowbird is our smallest blackbird and the only one with a brown head. The female, brownish-gray. Cowbirds walk when feeding, holding their tails higher than other blackbirds.— *Length: 7-8¼ in. Female smaller, brownish-gray all over.*

SCARLET TANAGER. Identification of this unmistakable bird is obvious. The female is a dull yellow-green, smaller in size, with a heavy bill and no wing bars. The Western Tanager (6½ in.) is bright yellow with red only on the head, and black wings, back, and tail. The male Summer Tanager (7½ in.) of the southeast is entirely red; the female is orange-yellow without wing bars; the extra large yellow bill of this bird is conspicuous.—*Length: 6½-7½ in. Female smaller, dull olive and yellow.*

CARDINAL. We have very few red birds — and the Cardinal is the only one with a crest. No other bird resembles it. Its heavy red bill with black around the base is a good field mark. The light-brown female Cardinal has the crest and red bill of the male, but very little of its red color. The Pyrrhuloxia (8 in.) of the southwest is a gray bird with a red face, crest, breast and tail and the general form of the Cardinal.— *Length: 7½-9¼ in. Female much duller.*

ROSE-BREASTED GROSBEAK. The male Rose-breasted Grosbeak, nearly all black and white, flashes a deep rose patch on its breast. Like all grosbeaks, it has a heavy, conical bill. The female is a mottled yellow-brown and white, like an overgrown sparrow. The Black-headed Grosbeak (7 in.) of the West has orange-brown under-parts, and black head and back. The Evening Grosbeak (8 in.) of the North is a brilliant metallic yellow with black-and-white wings and tail. —*Length: 7-8½ in. Female mottled yellow-brown.*

Black-headed   Rose-breasted

INDIGO BUNTING. This is our only small bird that is entirely blue. It lives in shrubbery and cut-over woods. The southern Blue Grosbeak (7 in.) is much larger, with chestnut bars on its wings. Other buntings are splashes of brilliant color. The Lazuli Bunting (5½ in.) of the West is similar to the Indigo, but has white bars on wings and a

chestnut breast. The male Painted Bunting (5 in.) of the South is a showy mixture of red, blue, and green; but the female is plain greenish above and yellowish below.—*Length: 5¼-5¾ in. Female and young uniform gray-brown.*

GOLDFINCH. The yellow body, black forehead and wings mark the Goldfinch. In the air, the Goldfinch is easily recognized by its roller-coaster flight and its clear song. It is a bird of fields and meadows, feeding and nesting near the ground. In the West, the Arkansas and the Green-backed Goldfinch (4 in.) are similar, with black crown, but darker (green to black) backs and duller yellow. Goldfinches are close rela-tives of our native sparrows and, like them, are birds of open weedy fields. —Length: 4½-6 in. Female and male in winter dull yellow-brown, with wing bars; no black on head.

PURPLE FINCH. These small, sparrowlike birds prefer pine woods and open canyons. The male is an old-rose color, hardly a purple, and the female—as dull as any sparrow—is hard to identify. The heavy bill, pale line over the eye, and sharply forked tail help distinguish it. These finches were more common in the East before the House Sparrows drove them out. In the West, the similar Purple Finch and Cassin Finch (6 in.) are hard to distinguish from the House Finch or Linnet (5½ in.), but the latter is grayer-crowned and has fine, dark streaking on the sides.—*Length: 5½-6¼ in. Female of similar pattern, but entirely brown and white.*

HOUSE FINCH. This bird is as common in some areas of the West as the House Sparrow is in the East. It is also a bird of farms, highways, and inhabited areas wherever water is available. The male has more brown on wings and breast than the Purple Finch. The forehead is more red than purple. The female is a nondescript, streaked bird, generally paler than the fe-male Purple Finch. The novice should be wary of both these females—at least as far as identification is con-cerned.—*Length: 5½-6 in. Female smaller, paler and duller.*

EASTERN TOWHEE. The Towhee may be identified by its "chewink" song and by its plumage. The black back and tail (white tip), white belly, and chestnut side patches are good field marks. The eyes are bright red, except in the southeast, where they become white. The western Spotted Towhee (8 in.) is similar to the eastern species, but with white spots on the wings and back. Towhees are ground birds, often seen scratching for insects in dead leaves. — *Length: 7½-8¾ in. Female smaller with brown instead of black.*

BROWN TOWHEE. This western Towhee is as plain brown a bird as any. It has traces of reddish-brown on the throat and under the tail. The shy Abert Towhee (8½ in.) of the desert is quite like the Brown Towhee but is more of a chestnut-brown, with a ring of black at the base of its bill. The Green-tailed Towhee (6½ in.) of western mountains is a green-backed bird with reddish crown, white throat, and gray underparts.—*Length: 8½-10 in. Female similar but duller.*

SLATE-COLORED JUNCO. This even-gray bird with clear white outer tail feathers is usually seen on the ground, feeding on seeds. The female Junco is browner and more sparrowlike. There are many similar western juncos, most of which cannot be safely identified in the field. Their heads are generally darker and they usually

Other Western Juncos

have a rusty streak on the side. The White-winged Junco (6½ in.) of the plains states is the only junco with two white wing bars.—*Length: 5¾-6½ in. Female smaller, browner.*

Chipping Sparrow

SPARROWS

The sparrow family also includes the finches, grosbeaks, buntings, and juncos. Altogether these make up the largest family of birds in the world and the largest family in this country, also. About 90 species have been recorded in North America. Some sparrows are very aggressive and adaptable birds. They seem to thrive in places where other birds find it hard to hold their own. The group is considered most "advanced" because sparrows are the most successful of the perching birds.

Sparrows are small to medium-sized, usually with stout, conical bills, well suited for crushing seeds, which are the principal item in the sparrows' diet. Seed eaters have a better chance for winter survival than insect eaters, so sparrows are common winter residents in areas where insect eaters cannot get food. Sparrows that live in the fields and near the ground are striped, brown and gray birds, easily concealed by their surroundings. They are fairly difficult for the beginner to identify. Tree-dwelling members of the family are likely to be more brightly colored. Some sparrows are good singers. The domesticated Canary (from the Canary Islands) is a member of the sparrow family.

FIELD SPARROW. This is a sparrow that displays a reddish-brown crown, but to clinch its identification look for

the plain breast, indistinct wing bars, and pink bill. No other small sparrow has this mark. It generally resembles the Chipping and Tree Sparrows—with which you should make comparisons. — *Length: 5-6 in. Female similar to male.*

TREE SPARROW. The combination that identifies the Tree Sparrow includes a large black spot in the center

of the grayish breast; two white wing bars; a reddish cap, and (upon close inspection) a bill that is dark above and yellow below.—*Length: 5¾-6½ in. Female and young similar.*

VESPER SPARROW. The white outer tail feathers are the distinguishing mark of the Vesper Sparrow. Otherwise the bird resembles the Song Sparrow. Other small birds with white outer tail feathers (pipits and juncos) are distinctly different. The Lark Sparrow (6 in.) of the West

is somewhat similar, but with a white fringe around the tail, a large, bright chestnut ear patch, and a single black breast spot.—*Length: 5½-6¾ in. Female and young similar.*

CHIPPING SPARROW. This small sparrow is equally common in the East and West. Its reddish crown, white line over the eye, black line through the eye, and black bill are good field marks. Breast not spotted or streaked. Of all the native sparrows, the Chipping is most fond

of inhabited areas, often nesting in hedges or shrubbery.—*Length: 5-5¾ in. Female similar. Young and adults have streaked crowns in fall.*

WHITE-CROWNED SPARROW. Here is a sparrow worth seeing. The black-and-white erect crown can't be missed. This, the erect posture, and the gray breast with no throat markings set the White-crowned Sparrow off as a handsome bird. The related Golden-crowned Sparrow

(6½ in.) of the Pacific states is similar, but with a dull-yellow crown bordered with black.—*Length: 6½-7½ in. Female similar; young with brown head stripes.*

WHITE-THROATED SPARROW. The crown of the White-Throated Sparrow is almost identical with that of the White-crowned, but you will also notice the yellow spot in front of the eye, which the White-crown lacks. Besides, as expected, the White-throat has a distinct,

white throat patch. It is the reputed "sweet singer" of the sparrows. Its whistled "Peabody" song is a familiar one.—*Length: 6¼-7¾ in. Female similar; young with brown head stripes and less yellow.*

SONG SPARROW. A large brown center spot on an otherwise streaked breast, and a rather long, rounded tail, which it pumps up and down as it flies, are the field marks of the Song Sparrow. Its melodious, varied song, heard most frequently in early spring, is easy to recognize. Song Sparrows are birds of hedgerows, shrubbery, and fields. The Lincoln Sparrow (5½ in.), most common in the

West, is similar but with a buff breast band crossed by fine dark streaks.—*Length: 6-6¾ in. Female similar to male; young with finer spotting.*

SWAMP SPARROW. For field identification note the Swamp Sparrow's white throat, red-brown crown, plain gray breast, and rounded tail. Other sparrows with this reddish crown are the Chipping, Field, and Tree. The

Swamp Sparrow is a stocky bird without wing bars. It lives, as its name implies, in swamps and along lake margins.—*Length: 4¾-5¾ in. Female similar; young duller.*

FOX SPARROW. A large sparrow, recognized in the field by its bright red-brown tail. Its breast is heavily spotted. Though somewhat similar to the Hermit Thrush in size and markings, the Fox Sparrow has a heavier bill and larger, browner breast markings. It is a bird of fields

and open clearings. The Fox Sparrow scratches in dry leaves with both feet at once like a Towhee.—*Length: 6¾-7½ in. Female and young similar.*

Page	Name	Migration*		Eggs	
		Arrive	Depart	Size (in.)	No.
21	Loon	DC*M-Oct B L-Sept SF M-Oct	WR M-May WR L-May WR E-May	3.5×2.2 Variable; greenish or dull brown with faint black spots.	2
22	Pied-billed Grebe	DC L-Mar B E-Apr StL M-Mar P Permanent Resident	SR L-Oct SR M-Oct SR L-Nov	1.7×1.1 Very light blue-green, darker or buff; unmarked.	4-8
23	Great Blue Heron	NY E-Apr B E-Apr StL L-Mar SF Permanent Resident	SR L-Nov SR M-Nov SR L-Oct	2.4×1.8 Pale bluish green to dull blue; unmarked.	3-4
24	Green Heron	DC M-Apr B L-Apr StL M-Apr SF M-Apr	SR L-Sept SR M-Sept SR L-Sept SR M-Sept	1.5×1.1 Pale greenish or greenish blue; unmarked.	3-6
25	Black-crowned Night Heron	B L-Mar StL L-Mar SF Permanent Resident P M-May	SR L-Nov SR E-Oct SR L-Sept	2.1×1.4 Pale bluish green.	3-5
26	Bittern	DC L-Mar NY M-Apr StL E-Apr P M-Apr	SR E-Nov SR L-Oct SR L-Oct SR M-Oct	2×1.5 Greenish, shading into buff; unmarked.	3-5
27	Canada Goose	DC M-Oct B L-Sept StL E-Oct P M-Sept	WR M-Apr Tr L-Apr WR M-Apr WR M-May	3.4×2.3 Cream to dull greenish white. Later buffy and mottled.	4-10
28	Mallard	DC E-Nov NY L-Oct StL M-Sept P Permanent Resident	WR M-Apr WR M-Apr WR L-Mar	2.3×1.6 Pale greenish to grayish buff.	6-12
29	Black Duck	DC Permanent Resident NY Permanent Resident B Permanent Resident StL L-Oct	WR E-Apr	2.3×1.7 Grayish white to greenish buff. Similar to Mallard.	6-12
30	Wood Duck	DC L-Feb NY M-Mar StL M-Feb P Permanent Resident	SR L-Nov SR E-Nov SR M-Nov	2×1.6 Dull cream to buff.	8-15

* See page 20 for full explanation of this material.

Nests		Food
Materials	Location	
Vegetable debris.	On ground, in hollows. Near shore, lake or pond.	Mainly fish; crabs, some insects and marine algae.
Decaying vegetation.	In shallow water. Floating among rushes in lakes and ponds.	Crayfish, crustaceans, small fish, and insects.
Sticks.	High up in tree or cliff near water.	Mainly fish; also crustaceans, frogs, and mice.
Sticks and twigs.	In trees, but near water; occasionally on ground.	Mainly fish; aquatic insects and crustaceans.
Sticks, twigs, and rushes.	In trees or rushes, in wooded swamps or islands.	Crayfish, fish, frogs, crabs, and insects.
Grasses and reeds.	On ground in marshes or wet grassy meadows.	Insects, frogs, crustaceans, fish; also mice.
Twigs, weeds, grasses, lined with down.	On dry ground near water.	Pondweeds, grasses; seeds of wheat, barley, sedges.
Reeds and grasses, lined with down.	On ground among high grass or reeds; usually near water.	Pondweeds, wild rice and other seeds; aquatic insects.
Grasses, weeds, leaves; feather lining.	Usually on ground in grass or brush. Often far from water.	Same as Mallard.
Grasses, twigs, leaves; down-lined.	Up to 60 ft. above ground; in a hole in tree or stump.	Wild rice, pondweeds, acorns, seeds, and fruits; some insects.

Page	Name	Migration*		Eggs	
		Arrive	Depart	Size (in.)	No.
31	Pintail	NY M-Sept StL L-Sept SF E-Sept P Permanent Resident	WR M-Apr Tr L-Apr WR M-Mar	2.2×1.5 Similar to Mallard.	5-12
32	Canvas-back	DC M-Oct NY M-Oct StL E-Mar SF M-Oct	WR L-Mar WR M-Apr Tr M-Dec WR L-Apr	2.5×1.6 Olive gray or dull green.	6-10
33	Merganser	DC L-Oct NY L-Oct B M-Oct P Permanent Resident	WR M-Apr WR L-Apr WR L-Apr	2.5×1.7 Pale buff; unmarked.	6-17
34	Coot	DC E-Oct NY E-Oct StL M-Feb SF Permanent Resident	WR M-May Tr L-Nov SR M-Nov	1.9×1.3 Light buff, speckled with dark brown or black.	8-12
35	Killdeer	NY M-Mar B L-Mar StL E-Mar SF Permanent Resident	SR E-Nov SR L-Oct SR L-Nov	1.5×1.1 Buff or darker; heavily spotted or mottled.	4
36	Wilson Snipe	DC M-Sept StL L-Feb SF M-Sept P Permanent Resident	Tr L-Apr Tr L-Nov WR E-May	1.6×1.2 Pale olive to brown; darker spots and specks.	4
37	Greater Yellow-legs	DC E-Apr NY E-Apr StL E-Apr SF E-Aug	Tr E-Nov Tr E-Nov Tr L-Oct Tr L-May	1.4×1.2 Grayish white; blotched with purple and brown.	3-4
38	Spotted Sandpiper	DC M-Apr B E-May StL M-Apr P L-Apr	SR L-Sept SR M-Sept SR E-Oct SR M-Oct	1.3×.9 White to cream; heav- ily marked with dark brown and black.	4
39	Least Sandpiper	DC E-May StL L-Apr SF L-July P E-May	Tr M-Oct Tr L-Oct WR L-Apr Tr L-Sept	1.2×.8 Pale brown or gray; marked with brown, gray, or black.	3-4
40	Herring Gull	DC M-Sept NY L-Aug StL M-Oct SF E-Nov	WR M-May WR L-May WR L-Apr WR M-Apr	2.9×1.9 Variable. Whitish to gray or brown; brown spots and blotches.	3-4

* See page 20 for full explanation of this material.

Nests		Food
Materials	Location	
Straw, grass, rushes; lined with down.	On dry ground in the open.	Rushes, pondweeds, seeds of aquatic plants; molluscs and insects.
Reeds, lined with down.	On ground in reeds or rushes, near water.	Wild celery, pondweeds plants; some molluscs, and other aquatic and aquatic insects.
Leaves, grasses, moss; lined with down.	On ground; beneath bushes and between boulders; or in a hole in a tree.	Fish, crayfish, frogs, occasional aquatic insects.
Heaps of reeds, rushes, and coarse grass.	On ground near water; sometimes half afloat.	Duckweeds and other aquatic plants. Molluscs, crustaceans, and aquatic insects.
Slight depression lined with pebbles, grasses, or debris.	A hollow in ground, in pastures or fields.	Mainly insects and earthworms; small crustaceans.
Slight depression lined with grass.	On ground or on slight elevation in meadows, open marshes, or bogs.	Insects, crustaceans, worms, seeds of swamp and aquatic plants.
Slight depression with little or no lining.	On ground along shores and in marshes.	Small fish, snails, worms, crustaceans, and some insects.
Slight depression lined with grasses.	On ground or cavity in rocks, on sandy or rocky shores. Banks of streams and open upland fields.	Mainly insects; worms, spiders, and small crustaceans.
Slight depression, sparingly lined with grass.	On ground or rock in grassy lowlands near water. Sometimes on moist upland.	Aquatic insects, worms, and small crustaceans.
Seaweeds; marsh plants, chips, feathers, shells. Sometimes no nest.	On ground. Birds nest in colonies. Often on islands; sometimes under heavy vegetation.	Small fish, molluscs, crustaceans, insects, garbage, blueberries.

Page	Name	Migration*		Eggs	
		Arrive	Depart	Size (in.)	No.
41	Common Tern	DC M-Apr NY L-Apr B E-May SF L-Apr	SR M-Oct SR M-Oct SR E-Oct SR M-Oct	1.6×1.2 Variable. Dull greenish white to brown; darker spots.	2-3
42	Cooper Hawk	NY M-Apr B M-Apr StL E-Apr SF Permanent Resident	Tr E-Oct SR E-Oct SR L-Oct	1.9×1.6 Bluish or greenish white; unmarked to heavily spotted with brown.	3-6
43	Red-tailed Hawk	Permanent Resident throughout its range, except in north central states		2.6×1.8 Dull or creamy white; spotted brown or purple; rarely unmarked.	2-4
44	Turkey Vulture	DC Permanent Resident NY L-Mar SF M-Mar P M-Mar	SR M-Nov SR L-Nov SR L-Sept	2.8×1.9 Dull white or buff; irregular brown spots.	1-3
45	Sparrow Hawk	Permanent Resident throughout its range, except in north central states		1.3×1.2 White or tinted with buff; spotted or speckled with brown.	4-7
46	Bald Eagle	Permanent Resident throughout its range		2.9×3.5 White; unmarked.	1-4
47	Osprey	DC M-Apr B L-Apr StL E-Apr SF M-Mar	SR M-Oct SR E-Oct SR L-Oct SR M-Oct	2.5×1.8 Variable. Dull white to buff or light brown with brown blotches.	2-4
48	Ring-necked Pheasant	Permanent Resident throughout its range		1.8×1.4 Buff to dark olive; occasionally greenish.	6-16
49	Ruffed Grouse	Permanent Resident throughout its range		1.5×1.1 Pale buff but varying in color; unmarked.	8-14
50	Bob-white	Permanent Resident throughout its range		1.2×1.0 White; unmarked.	10-24

* See page 20 for full explanation of this material.

Nests		Food
Materials	Location	
Hollow, lined with shells, to well-built mound of grass and seaweed.	On sand or bare rock, sometimes among grasses. Usually on islands.	Feeds almost wholly on small fish, but also some insects.
Branches and twigs; often lined with bark.	Usually in trees: pines preferred, 25-65 ft. high. Rarely on ground.	Mainly wild birds and poultry; some mammals; other vertebrates and insects.
Branches and twigs; lined with grasses, weeds, dead leaves.	In tall trees, 20-80 ft. up; in forest areas or in small groves.	Mainly rodents; some reptiles and poultry.
None.	On ground, rock ledge, or hollow log in secluded places, near water or in woods.	Carrion.
No nest material, unless some was left by previous occupant.	In cavity of tree, cliff embankment, 7-80 ft. up; often in farms or orchards.	Largely insects, some rodents, lizards, and small birds.
Large nest of branches and sticks. Additions and repairs are made yearly.	In treetops or cliffs; 30-90 ft. up; in forested or wooded regions, near streams, lakes, or ocean.	Mostly fish; some rodents and a few birds.
Platform of sticks; additions made from year to year.	In trees: 15-50 ft. up or on rocks. Ospreys nest along coasts.	Almost entirely fish.
Dead leaves, grass, straw.	On ground in bushy pastures, moorlands, grass, and grain fields.	Corn, wheat, barley, wild fruits, and insects.
Shallow depression, lined with leaves.	On ground, at base of tree in wooded uplands or dense thicket; under logs.	Leaves, buds, and fruits of forest plants. Occasional insects.
Grass, stems, strips of bark.	On ground in grass tangles, open fields, hedgerows.	Corn and grain. Ragweed, lespedeza, acorns, and weed seeds.

Page	Name	Migration*		Eggs	
		Arrive	Depart	Size (in.)	No.
51	Pigeon	Permanent Resident throughout its range		1.5×1.1 White; unmarked.	2-3
52	Mourning Dove	DC Permanent Resident NY M-Mar SR M-Nov B L-Mar SR L-Oct SF L-Mar SR M-Nov		1.1×.8 White; unmarked.	2
53	Screech Owl	Permanent Resident throughout its range		1.4×1.3 White; unmarked.	3-5
54	Barn Owl	Permanent Resident throughout its range		1.6×1.2 White; unmarked.	5-11
55	Horned Owl	Permanent Resident throughout its range		2.3×1.9 Rough white; unmarked.	2-3
56	Yellow-billed Cuckoo	DC E-May SR M-Sept NY E-May SR L-Sept StL L-May SR L-Sept SF L-May SR E-Aug		1.2×.9 Light bluish green; unmarked; occasionally mottled.	2-4
57	Chimney Swift	DC M-Apr SR E-Oct B L-Apr SR E-Sept StL E-Apr SR M-Oct		.8×.5 White; unmarked.	4-5
58	Whip-poor-will	DC M-Apr SR L-Sept B E-May SR M-Sept StL M-Apr SR E-Oct		1.2×.8 Creamy white; spotted with brown.	2
59	Nighthawk	DC E-May SR L-Sept B M-May SR M-Sept StL L-Apr SR E-Oct P E-June SR L-Sept		1.2×.9 Dull white; spotted with gray and brown.	2
60	Ruby-throated Hummingbird	DC E-May SR L-Sept NY M-May SR M-Sept StL L-Apr SR E-Oct		.5×.4 White; unmarked.	2

* See page 20 for full explanation of this material.

Nests		Food
Materials	Location	
Sticks, straw, and debris.	Building (30 ft. and higher), on sheltered eaves or ledge.	Corn, oats, weed seeds, farm gleanings.
Stems, straws, sometimes leaves and moss.	In trees (pines preferred) 2-45 ft. above ground; in upland, sometimes in wet lowlands.	Wheat, corn, grass, and weed seeds.
No nest; or uses any available material.	Hollow of tree (5-50 ft. up), cranny, nook of building.	Rodents, small birds, frogs, fish, and insects.
Sometimes rubbish or debris. Usually no nest.	Underground in burrows or holes in embankments. Or elevated nests of other birds; steeples, barns.	Mice, rats, gophers, and some birds.
Sometimes uses old hawk nests; sometimes none.	In large trees (preferably pines) 10-90 ft. up. Sometimes in tree hollow or even on ground.	Rabbits, squirrels, rats, wild birds and poultry.
Sticks, rootlets, straws, pine needles, lichens.	In trees or thickets, 3-20 ft. up. Prefers margins of woods, orchards, or thickets.	Insects, mostly caterpillars, including hairy species.
Coarse twigs, held together by saliva of bird.	Usually near top of chimneys or rarely in barns or sheds; sometimes inside wells.	Flies, mosquitoes, and other small insects, caught in flight.
No nest construction. Uses slight depression in leaves.	On ground, usually in brushy wood margins, on well-drained land.	Moths, flying ants, and other insects caught in flight.
None. Eggs laid on bare surface.	On ground, rock, or on flat roofs of building; in open fields, pastures, or city lots.	Similar to Whip-poor-will.
Plant-down, bits of lichen outside; bound by threads of saliva and spider web.	Placed or "saddled" on branch of tree—3-50 ft. above ground.	Nectar of flowers and small insects.

Page	Name	Migration*		Eggs	
		Arrive	Depart	Size (in.)	No.
61	Belted Kingfisher	DC L-Mar B E-Apr StL L-Feb SF M-Mar	SR E-Nov SR L-Oct SR L-Nov SR M-Nov	1.3×1.0 Glossy white; unmarked.	5-8
62	Red-headed Woodpecker	DC Permanent Resident NY E-May StL E-Apr	Tr L-Sept SR E-Oct	1.0×.8 White; unmarked.	4-6
63	Flicker	DC Permanent Resident NY M-Mar B M-Apr SF Permanent Resident	SR L-Oct SR M-Oct	1.1×.9 Glossy white; unmarked.	5-9
64	Yellow-bellied Sapsucker	DC E-Oct B M-Apr StL M-Mar SF M-Oct	WR M-Apr Tr L-Oct Tr M-Nov WR M-Mar	.9×.7 Glossy white; unmarked.	5-7
65	Downy Woodpecker	Permanent Resident throughout its range		.8×.6 White; unmarked.	4-6
66	Kingbird	DC L-Apr NY E-May StL M-Apr P M-May	SR E-Sept SR E-Sept SR M-Sept SR M-Sept	1.0×.7 Creamy white, spotted with brown.	3-4
67	Crested Flycatcher	DC E-May B M-May StL E-May	SR M-Sept SR E-Sept SR M-Sept	.9×.7 Creamy, streaked with brown.	3-6
68	Phoebe	DC M-Mar NY M-Mar StL E-Mar	SR M-Oct SR M-Oct SR M-Oct	.8×.6 White; occasionally spotted with brown.	4-5
69	Least Flycatcher	DC E-May B E-May StL E-May	Tr M-Sept SR E-Sept Tr E-Oct	.6×.5 White; unmarked.	3-4
70	Horned Lark	Permanent Resident throughout its range		.8×.6 Dull white; speckled with brown or purple.	3-5

* See page 20 for full explanation of this material.

Nests		Food
Materials	Location	
Nest lined with fish-bones and scales, leaves, grass.	At end of burrow in bank or bluff. Usually not more than 10 ft. up. Usually near water.	Mainly fish; some crustaceans and frogs.
A gourd-shaped hole, padded with chips.	Excavations in trees, posts, poles: 5-80 ft. up.	Beetles, ants, other insects. Acorns, other wild fruits and seeds.
Hole, padded with chips.	Cavity 10-24 in. deep in trees, snags, poles: 6 in.-60 ft. high.	Ants, beetles, and other insects. Wild fruits and seeds.
Hole, lined with chips.	Cavity in dead or live tree 8-40 ft. up; in woods or orchards.	Ants, beetles, other insects and their eggs. Wood and sap; wild fruits.
Gourd-shaped excavation: 6-10 in. deep.	In dead limb 5-50 ft. up; woodlands, orchards.	Ants and boring insects, spiders, snails. Some fruits and seeds.
Rootlets, grass, twine, hair, wool. Lined with fine grass, moss.	On horizontal limb of tree; bushes, eaves, fence rails, bridges: 2-60 ft. up.	Bees, ants, grasshoppers, beetles, etc. Also some wild fruits.
Twigs, grass, leaves, moss, feathers, and usually a cast-off snakeskin.	Cavity in dead limb or post. Sometimes buildings; 3-70 ft. up.	Moths, grasshoppers, other flying insects. Occasional fruits.
Of mud, covered with moss and dead leaves, lined with grass rootlets, moss, feathers.	In shelter of undercut banks, tree roots, culverts, eaves, or inside farm buildings; 1-20 ft. up.	Flying insects: beetles, flies, moths, etc. Some wild fruit; few seeds.
Grasses, bark fibers, lined with feathers and other soft materials.	Fork of tree or upright twigs: 2-60 ft. up. Usually along wood margins.	Small insects: flies, mosquitoes, moths, beetles.
Depression, loosely filled with grass, fibers, feathers.	On ground, in cultivated fields, sand dunes, or barren islands; in cover of grass and moss.	Mixed diet of insects and (in winter) seeds of weeds and grasses.

Page	Name	Migration*		Eggs	
		Arrive	Depart	Size (in.)	No.
71	Purple Martin	DC L-Mar NY M-Apr StL L-Mar	SR M-Sept Tr L-Aug SR M-Sept	1.0×.7 White; unmarked.	4-5
72	Tree Swallow	DC M-Apr B M-Apr StL M-Mar SF E-Mar	Tr L-Sept SR M-Sept SR E-Oct SR M-Sept	.7×.6 White; unmarked.	4-7
73	Barn Swallow	NY M-Apr StL E-Apr SF L-Mar P M-Apr	SR M-Sept SR E-Oct SR E-Sept SR L-Sept	.8×.5 White, spotted with brown.	3-6
74	Magpie	Permanent Resident throughout its range		1.3×.9 Grayish, heavily marked with brown.	4-8
75	Crow	Permanent Resident throughout its range		1.6×1.2 Variable. Pale greenish or bluish, spotted or blotched with brown.	3-5
76	Blue Jay	Permanent Resident throughout its range		1.1×.9 Greenish to olive, spotted with brown.	4-6
77	White-breasted Nuthatch	Permanent Resident throughout its range		.8×.6 White, rarely pinkish; speckled or spotted with brown.	5-8
78	Black-capped Chickadee	Permanent Resident throughout its range		.6×.5 White, finely spotted with brown.	5-8
79	Tufted Titmouse	Permanent Resident throughout its range		.7×.6 White to buff; speckled with grayish brown.	5-8
80	Brown Creeper	DC E-Oct NY L-Sept StL L-Sept SF Permanent Resident	WR L-Apr WR E-May WR L-Apr	.6×.5 White, speckled with brown.	5-8

* See page 20 for full explanation of this material.

Nests		Food
Materials	Location	
Leaves, grass, straw, twigs.	In cavities of trees, holes in cliffs: 3-30 ft. high. Frequently uses bird-houses.	Flying insects: flies, bees, beetles, flying ants, moths, etc.
Grass, lining of feathers.	Hollows and cavities in trees, woodpecker holes, crevices in buildings; also birdhouses; 2-50 ft. up.	Flies, moths, bees, bee-tles and other flying insects. Uses bayberries as a winter food.
Mud reinforced with plant material. Lined with feathers.	Commonly in barns; hol-lows in trees, cliffs; 5-20 ft. up. Adheres to an up-right surface.	Entirely flying insects: flies, bees, ants, bee-tles.
Large nest of sticks and mud; lining of rootlets or horsehair.	In bushes and trees: 8-30 ft. up.	Grasshoppers; other in-sects, carrion, small mammals; wild and cul-tivated fruits.
Twigs and sticks, lined with rootlets, vines, grass.	In trees (preferably pine woods), height 10-70 ft.	Corn and other grains, weed seeds, wild fruits; grasshoppers and other insects.
Twigs and rootlets, lined with grass, feathers.	In a fork of tree: 5-50 ft. up. Prefers evergreen for-ests. But often in suburbs, farms, and villages.	Acorns, beechnuts, corn and other grain. Some insects, eggs, and young birds.
Grass, plant fibers, twigs, hair, and feathers.	A cavity or deserted woodpecker hole: 5-60 ft. up. Mature trees pre-ferred.	Beetles, ants, other in-sects and their eggs. A few seeds.
Moss, hair, feathers, grass; lined with plant down.	Cavity in rotted stump or limb: 1-50 ft. up; or de-serted woodpecker hole.	Insects and their eggs, weed and tree seeds; wild fruits.
Leaves, moss, bark; lined with feathers.	Deserted woodpeckers' holes or stumps: 2-85 ft. up.	Ants, bugs, and other insects; some seeds and fruits.
Twigs, plant fibers; sometimes lined with spider web, feathers, or hair.	In trees, behind or be-tween loose strip of bark: 5-15 ft. up. Usually in deep woods.	Mainly insects: beetles, bugs, caterpillars, ants, etc.

Page	Name	Migration*		Eggs	
		Arrive	Depart	Size (in.)	No.
81	House Wren	DC M-Apr NY L-Apr StL M-Apr SF E-Mar	SR M-Oct SR E-Oct SR M-Oct SR M-Sept	.7×.5 Dull white, densely spotted with brown.	5-10
82	Mockingbird	DC Permanent Resident StL E-Mar SR L-Oct SF M-Sept WR M-Apr (Permanent Res. in S. Calif.)		1.0×.8 Greenish to blue; spot- ted brown, mostly at large end.	3-6
83	Catbird	DC L-Apr NY E-May StL L-Apr	SR M-Oct SR E-Oct SR M-Oct	.9×.7 Deep greenish blue or bluish green; unmarked.	4-6
84	Brown Thrasher	DC E-Apr NY L-Apr B L-Apr StL M-Mar	SR L-Sept SR L-Sept SR M-Sept SR E-Oct	1.1×.8 Grayish or greenish white; thickly spotted with brown.	3-6
85	Robin	DC Permanent Resident NY E-Mar SR M-Nov StL Permanent Resident SF E-Nov WR L-Mar		1.2×.8 Greenish blue; ra spotted.	
86	Wood Thrush	NY E-May B M-May StL M-Apr	SR E-Oct SR M-Sept SR M-Oct	1.1×.8 Bright greenish bl unmarked.	
87	Hermit Thrush	DC L-Oct NY E-Apr B M-Apr SF M-Oct	WR L-Apr SR M-Nov SR E-Nov WR E-Apr	.9×.7 Greenish blue; u marked.	3
88	Bluebird	DC Permanent Resident NY M-Mar SR M-Nov StL L-Feb SR L-Nov P Permanent Resident		.9×.7 Pale blue; rarely whi unmarked.	4
89	Blue-gray Gnatcatcher	DC M-Apr NY L-Apr StL L-Mar SF Permanent Resident	SR E-Sept SR E-Sept SR M-Sept	.6×.5 White or bluish white speckled with brown.	4
90	Golden-crowned Kinglet	DC L-Sept NY L-Sept StL L-Mar SF L-Oct	WR M-Apr WR M-Apr Tr L-Oct WR E-Mar	.6×.4 White to cream; spott with pale brown.	5-7

* See page 20 for full explanation of this material.

Nests		Food
Materials	Location	
Twigs, stems, grasses, lined with feathers, hair.	A cavity in hollow tree: 5-60 ft. up. Woodlands, farmyards, and in cities. Bird boxes commonly used.	Small insects: bugs, beetles, caterpillars, etc.
Bulky nest of coarse twigs, weed stems, shreds, string, rags.	In shrubs, thickets, vines; near houses; 1-15 ft., rarely higher.	Beetles, grasshoppers, and other insects; some wild fruit in season—grape and holly preferred.
Twigs and leaves. Lined with bark shreds, rootlets.	In shrubbery, thicket: 1-10 ft. and rarely 25 ft. high. Prefers dense lowlands.	Food similar to Mockingbird.
Bulky nest of coarse twigs, weed stalks, leaves. Lined with rootlets, grass.	In bushes, vines, brush, and low trees. Height: 0-12 ft.	Beetles, grasshoppers, caterpillars, etc. Also some acorns and wild fruit.
Mud wall and bottom, reinforced with grass, twine, twigs. Lined with grass.	In tree crotch or among branches: 5-70 ft. up. In woods or open country. On buildings, in rural areas.	Garden and field insects, worms; cultivated and wild fruits. Some seeds.
Leaves, rootlets, fine twigs. Firmly woven, with inner wall of mud.	Usually in saplings in woods. Height: 3-40 ft.	Beetles, ants, caterpillars, and other insects. Some wild fruits and weed seeds.
Moss, grasses, leaves. Lined with rootlets and pine needles.	On or near ground in pine or hemlock woods.	Food similar to Woodthrush.
Grasses, rootlets, hair, and some feathers.	In hollow trees, deserted woodpecker holes, and birdhouses. Height: 3-30 ft.	Many insects, including beetles, weevils, and grasshoppers. Also holly, dogwood, and other wild fruits.
Tendrils, fine bark, and grasses. Firmly woven and covered with lichens.	On a branch or in a crotch in tree near water. Height: 10-70 ft.	Mainly small insects: beetles, flies, caterpillars, moths.
Green mosses, lined with fine inner bark, black rootlets, and feathers.	In coniferous trees, partly suspended from twigs: 4-60 ft. up.	Insects: flies, beetles, plant lice; insect eggs.

Page	Name	Migration*		Eggs	
		Arrive	Depart	Size (in.)	No.
91	Ruby-crowned Kinglet	NY E-Apr B M-Apr StL E-Oct P M-Apr	Tr M-Oct Tr M-Oct Tr L-Apr SR M-Oct	.5×.4 White to cream. Similar to Golden-crowned Kinglet.	4-9
92	Cedar Waxwing	DC M-Sept NY M-May P Permanent Resident	WR E-June SR M-Nov	.9×.6 Grayish blue; speckled brown or black; mostly at large end.	3-5
93	Loggerhead Shrike	NY E-Aug B M-Mar StL Permanent Resident SF Permanent Resident	Tr E-Oct Tr L-Oct	1.0×.8 Dull white; spotted and blotched with light brown.	3-5
94	Starling	Permanent Resident throughout its range, except in extreme North		1.2×.9 Whitish or pale blue; unmarked.	4-6
96	Yellow Warbler	DC L-Apr NY E-May StL L-Apr SF M-Apr	SR E-Sept SR L-Aug SR M-Sept SR E-Sept	.7×.5 Pale bluish white; brown spots forming ring at larger end.	4-5
96	Black and White Warbler	DC M-Apr NY L-Apr StL M-Apr	SR L-Sept SR M-Sept SR L-Sept	.7×.5 Greenish white to buff; spotted and blotched with brown.	4-5
96	Black-throated Blue Warbler	NY E-May B M-May StL E-May	Tr L-Sept Tr M-Sept Tr M-Sept	.7×.5 Creamy white; speckled with brown and lavender; mostly at larger end.	3-5
98	Yellow-throat	DC L-Apr NY E-May StL M-Mar SF Permanent Resident	SR E-Oct SR M-Oct SR E-Oct	.7×.5 Creamy white; speckled with brown and black; chiefly at large end.	3-5
98	Water-thrush	DC E-May B M-May StL L-Apr	Tr M-Sept Tr L-Sept Tr L-Sept	.8×.6 White to creamy; spotted with brown and gray.	4-5
98	Oven-bird	DC L-Apr NY E-May StL L-Apr	SR L-Sept SR M-Sept SR E-Oct	.8×.6 White, spotted with brown, especially at larger end.	4-6

* See page 20 for full explanation of this material.

Nests		Food
Materials	**Location**	
Plant down, covered by mosses and lichens. Bound with plant fibers.	In conifers, often saddled on a limb; 5-50 ft. up.	Ants, plant lice, scale insects, and insect eggs. Occasional use of wild fruits.
Bulky nest of bark, leaves, grasses, rootlets, moss, and sometimes mud.	Often in fruit and shade trees at height of 5-50 ft.	Wild and cultivated fruits: grapes, dogwood, hawthorn, cherries; some insects.
Strips of bark, small twigs, and vegetable fibers; lined with grasses.	In thorny hedges or low trees: 5-20 ft. up.	Insects; grasshoppers, beetles; some small rodents and birds.
Large, poorly built nest of grasses and twigs.	In hollow of tree or crevice of building; 3-40 ft. high. Uses bird boxes.	Beetles, grasshoppers, and other insects; wild and cultivated fruits and grain.
Fine grasses and fibers; lined with plant down, fine grass, some hair.	In shrubs and trees: 3-8 ft. up. Rarely 40 ft. Fields and orchards, near water.	Caterpillars, weevils, and other small insects. Slight amount of plant food.
Strips of fine bark, grasses; lined with rootlets or hairs.	On ground, at base of trees, logs, or rocks.	Plant lice, caterpillars, beetles, scale and other insects.
Bark, fine grasses, pine needles. Lining of black rootlets.	In heavy undergrowth of dense woods: 1-10 ft. above ground.	Mainly insects: caterpillars, small beetles, plant lice, etc.
Bark, coarse grasses, dead leaves. Lined with fine grass tendrils.	On or near ground. Usually in clump of grass, in moist location.	Insects: cankerworms, weevils, leafhoppers, caterpillars, etc.
Moss, lined with tendrils and fine rootlets.	On ground in a mossy bank or under roots of fallen tree.	Insects: beetles, bugs, caterpillars, leafhoppers, and spiders.
Bulky, covered nest. Entrance at one side. Of leaves, coarse grasses, and rootlets.	On leaf-covered ground in open woods.	Beetles, grasshoppers, and other ground insects. Worms and spiders.

Page	Name	Migration*		Eggs	
		Arrive	Depart	Size (in.)	No.
100	Myrtle Warbler	NY L-Sept StL E-Apr SF L-Oct	WR E-May Tr L-Oct WR M-Apr	.7×.5 White, speckled with brown; often forming ring at larger end.	4-5
100	Redstart	DC L-Apr B E-May StL L-Apr	SR M-Sept SR M-Sept SR M-Sept	.7×.5 Bluish white; brown spots occasionally ringing large end.	4-5
100	Wilson Warbler	DC E-May NY M-May SF L-Mar	Tr L-Sept Tr M-Sept SR E-Sept	.7×.5 White or pinkish; brown spots forming ring at larger end.	4-5
102	Red-eyed Vireo	NY M-May B M-May StL M-Apr P E-May	SR L-Sept SR M-Sept SR E-Oct SR L-Sept	.9×.6 White, sparsely speckled with brown or black.	3-4
103	House Sparrow	Permanent Resident throughout its range		.9×.6 White to dull brown; speckled with brown.	4-7
104	Bobolink	DC E-May B M-May StL E-May P L-May	Tr L-Sept SR M-Sept Tr L-Sept SR M-Sept	.9×.6 Dull white; spotted and blotched with brown and gray.	4-7
105	Meadowlark	NY M-Mar B L-Mar StL M-Mar SF Permanent Resident	SR L-Oct SR L-Oct SR L-Oct	1.1×.8 White; completely spotted and speckled with brown.	3-7
106	Brewer Blackbird	StL M-Mar SF Permanent Resident P Permanent Resident	Tr E-Apr	1.0×.8 Dull white; almost entirely spotted with brown and black.	4-7
107	Red-wing	DC M-Mar NY M-Mar StL E-Mar SF Permanent Resident	SR M-Nov SR L-Oct SR E-Nov	1.0×.7 Bluish white; irregular spots and streaks of purple and black.	3-5
108	Baltimore Oriole	DC E-May NY M-May StL L-Apr	Tr E-Sept SR E-Sept SR E-Sept	.9×.6 White; irregular streaks and blotches of brown and black.	4-6

* See page 20 for full explanation of this material.

Nests		Food
Materials	**Location**	
Plant fibers; lining of grasses.	Coniferous trees in heavy woods: 5-40 ft. high.	Mainly common insects, but takes poison ivy, bayberry, and other fruits in winter.
Bark, leafstalks, plant down. Firmly woven and lined with rootlets.	Usually in the crotch of a sapling: 3-30 ft. above ground, rarely higher.	Small insects: flies, beetles, moths, leafhoppers, etc.
Ball of grass and moss wrapped in leaves. Lined with fine rootlets.	On ground among bushes in swampy land.	Small insects, similar to other warblers. Makes slight use of plant food.
Strips of bark, paper, plant down. Firmly and smoothly woven. Lined with bark and tendrils.	Suspended from a forked branch: 3-75 ft. up.	Caterpillars, moths, bugs, beetles, and other insects; small amount of wild fruit.
Of any available material: string, straw, twigs, paper, etc.	In any available place: in buildings, structures, eaves. Height: over 5 ft.	Corn, oats, wheat, and other grain; weed seeds; some insects during spring and summer.
Nest of grasses, weed stems, and rootlets.	On ground in the tall meadow grasses.	Wild rice, cultivated grains, weed seeds, caterpillars and other insects.
Grasses and weeds; often arched over.	Usually on ground in grassy fields or meadows.	Grain and wild grass seeds, wild fruits, grasshoppers, and other insects.
Twigs and coarse grass. Lined with finer grass.	On ground or in shrubs or coniferous trees. Height: 0-10 ft.	Oats and other grain, weed seeds, some insects.
Coarse grasses and weeds. Lined with finer grass and rootlets.	Attached to low bushes, reeds; usually in swamps. Usually less than 15 ft. high.	Weed and marsh plant seeds, grain; some fruit and insects in season.
Grasses, plant fibers, hair, strings, etc. Firmly interwoven.	Hanging from end of branches in shade or fruit trees. Height: 10-90 ft.	Caterpillars, beetles, and other insects; wild and some cultivated fruits.

Page	Name	Migration*		Eggs	
		Arrive	Depart	Size (in.)	No.
109	Grackle	DC L-Feb NY E-Mar StL E-Mar	SR L-Nov SR E-Nov SR M-Nov	1.2×.8 Bluish white; speckled and spotted dark brown to black.	3-7
110	Cowbird	DC E-Mar NY M-Mar StL E-Mar P E-May	SR E-Nov SR M-Oct SR M-Nov SR L-Sept	.9×.7 White or bluish; heavily speckled with gray or brown.	4-5
111	Scarlet Tanager	DC E-May B M-May StL L-Apr	SR L-Sept SR M-Sept SR E-Oct	.9×.7 Pale greenish or bluish; speckled brown at larger end.	3-4
112	Cardinal	Permanent Resident over much of its range		1.0×.7 Pale bluish white; finely spotted with reddish brown.	3-4
113	Rose-breasted Grosbeak	DC E-May NY M-May StL L-Apr	Tr L-Sept SR M-Sept SR E-Oct	.9×.7 Pale blue; spotted with brown.	4-5
114	Indigo Bunting	DC L-Apr B M-May StL L-Apr	SR E-Oct SR M-Sept SR E-Oct	.7×.6 Pale bluish white; unmarked.	3-4
115	Goldfinch	Permanent Resident		.7×.5 Pale bluish white; unmarked.	3-6
116	Purple Finch	DC L-Oct NY L-Mar StL L-Mar SF Permanent Resident	WR M-Apr Tr E-Nov Tr E-Nov	.8×.6 Blue; spotted and speckled with brown at larger end.	4-6
117	House Finch	Permanent Resident		.8×.6 Pale blue, nearly white; thinly speckled with black.	3-5
118	Eastern Towhee	NY M-Apr B L-Apr StL L-Mar	SR E-Oct SR E-Oct SR M-Oct	1.0×.7 White or pinkish; brown specks at large end.	4-5

* See page 20 for full explanation of this material.

Nests		Food
Materials	Location	
Bulky, but compact. Of mud and coarse grasses; lined with finer grasses.	Nests in colonies, most often in coniferous trees; sometimes in bushes. Height: 5-80 ft.	Grain and weed seeds. Some wild fruit; beetles, grasshoppers, crickets, etc.
None added.	Eggs laid in nests of other birds. Usually 1 or 2 in any one nest.	Grain and weed seeds. Grasshoppers and other insects.
Fine twigs and weeds. Lined with vine tendrils and stems.	On horizontal limb, often near its end: 10-70 ft. up.	Mainly insects: ants, beetles, moths, caterpillars. Dogwood, blackberry, and other wild fruits.
Twigs, rootlets, strips of bark. Lined with grasses and rootlets.	In thick bushes or vines: 2-10 ft. high. Rarely up to 30 ft.	Grape, holly, blackberry; wild seeds and a good many kinds of insects.
Loose nest of fine twigs, weeds, rootlets.	In trees or bushes: 5-20 ft. high.	Insects, including beetles, caterpillars, ants, bees. Wild fruits when available.
Grasses, bits of dead leaves, bark; lined with fine grass, rootlets, hairs.	In crotch of bush or sapling: 1-10 ft. up. Rarely as high as 20 ft.	Diet mixed: caterpillars and other insects; some wild fruits, weed seeds.
Fine grasses, bark, moss; thickly lined with thistledown.	In trees or bushes: 5-35 ft. high.	Mainly weed seeds, grain, and wild fruit. Occasional plant lice and caterpillars.
Twigs, grasses, and rootlets. Thickly lined with hairs.	Woods, in pine and spruce trees: 5-60 ft. high.	Tree seeds and wild fruits. Some insects.
Rootlets and grasses. Lined with horsehair.	Trees, bushes, and vines: 5-20 ft. above ground. Often near buildings.	Weed seeds, tree seeds, plant lice and other insects.
Dead leaves and bark; lined with fine grasses.	Usually on ground; sometimes in bushes or saplings: 0-10 ft. high.	Wild fruits and weed seeds. Insects, worms, and spiders.

Page	Name	Migration*		Eggs	
		Arrive	Depart	Size (in.)	No.
119	Brown Towhee	Permanent Resident in its range		1.0×.7 Variable; bluish marked with purple and black.	3-4
120	Slate-colored Junco	DC E-Oct NY L-Sept P E-Oct	WR L-Apr WR L-Apr WR M-Mar	.8×.6 Pale bluish white; brown spots may form ring at larger end.	4-5
122	Field Sparrow	NY M-Apr B M-Apr StL L-Mar	SR L-Oct SR M-Oct SR E-Nov	.7×.5 White to pale blue or green; speckled with brown.	3-5
122	Tree Sparrow	NY E-Nov B L-Oct StL L-Oct P L-Oct	WR L-Mar WR E-Apr WR L-Mar WR M-Mar	.8×.6 Pale greenish or bluish green; speckled with light brown.	4-5
122	Vesper Sparrow	DC L-Mar B M-Apr StL L-Mar P E-Apr	SR L-Oct SR M-Oct Tr M-Nov SR M-Sept	.9×.6 Dull white; thickly spotted with brown.	4-5
124	Chipping Sparrow	DC L-Mar B M-Apr StL L-Mar SF M-Apr	SR E-Nov SR M-Oct SR L-Oct SR M-Sept	.7×.5 Greenish blue; speckled with brown, mostly at larger end.	4-5
124	White-crowned Sparrow	DC E-May NY M-May StL L-Apr Permanent Resident	Tr M-Nov Tr L-Oct Tr E-Nov	.9×.6 Bluish and greenish white, spotted with brown.	4-5
124	White-throated Sparrow	DC M-Oct NY E-Oct StL M-Oct	WR M-May Tr M-May Tr M-May	.8×.6 White to bluish; speckled and blotched with reddish brown.	4-5
126	Song Sparrow	Permanent Resident over much of its range		.8×.6 Variable. White or greenish; spotted and speckled with brown.	4-5
126	Swamp Sparrow	DC E-Oct B M-Apr StL L-Mar	WR E-May SR M-Oct Tr L-Oct	.8×.6 Bluish white; spotted or blotched with brown.	4-5
126	Fox Sparrow	DC L-Oct NY L-Oct StL L-Oct SF E-Oct	Tr L-Mar Tr E-Apr Tr E-Apr WR E-Apr	.8×.6 Greenish white; spotted with dull brown.	4-5

* See page 20 for full explanation of this material.

Nests		Food
Materials	Location	
Grasses, weeds, and twigs. Lined with rootlets.	On ground or in low bushes. Less than 10 ft. high.	Oats and barley; weed seeds, caterpillars and other insects.
Grasses, moss, and rootlets. Lined with fine grass and hair.	On or very near ground in fallen tree, logs, up-turned roots; under over-hanging banks, along wood roads.	Ragweed, crabgrass, and other weed seeds. Some caterpillars and other insects.
Coarse grasses, weeds, rootlets. Lined with fine grass and hairs.	On ground or low bushes (10 ft. or less) in fields, overgrown pastures.	Similar to Tree Spar-row, with some use of grain.
Grasses, rootlets, and hair.	On ground or in stunted conifers near timberline; near water.	Largely weed seeds; crabgrass, pigweed, sedge, etc. Some insects eaten.
Coarse grass. Lined with finer grasses, rootlets, hairs.	On ground in dry upland fields; along dry road-sides.	Weed seeds of many kinds; some grain, and various insects.
Grasses, fine twigs, rootlets. Thickly lined with hair.	In trees or bushes; in shrubbery near houses. Height: 3-35 ft. Rarely on ground.	Weed seeds, oats, and timothy; leafhoppers and other common insects.
Grasses, moss, and rootlets. Lined with hair.	Usually on ground or in clump of grass in woods or thickets.	Ragweed, pigweed, knotweed, and other weed seeds; some grain and a number of kinds of insects.
Grasses, rootlets, moss, strips of bark. Lined with finer grasses.	Usually on ground in hedgerows and woodland undergrowth.	Food very similar to White-crowned Spar-row.
Nest of grasses and rootlets. Lined with fine grasses and hair.	On ground or in low bushes; in grass thickets or saplings. Up to 8 ft.; rarely 15 ft.	Food similar to that of Swamp Sparrow.
Coarse grasses, root-lets, dead leaves. Lined with finer grass-es and sometimes hair.	On or close to ground; in grasses in wet meadow and marshes or swamps.	Seeds of weeds and grasses. Beetles, cater-pillars, and other in-sects.
Coarse grasses. Lined with finer grasses, hair, mosses, feath-ers.	On ground or in low bushes; coniferous for-ests or alder thickets pre-ferred.	Weed seeds, wild fruits, some grain, millipedes, and various insects.

OTHER BOOKS TO USE

This field guide will help you to use more advanced books successfully. Here are a few of the best:

A Field Guide to the Birds and *A Field Guide to Western Birds* by Roger T. Peterson (Houghton Mifflin). Excellent guides, emphasizing field markings and outlines of birds in flight. The revised *Eastern Guide* is the bird watchers' bible.

A Guide to Bird Watching by Joseph J. Hickey (Oxford Univ. Press). A most helpful book with practical details on what the amateur can do and how to do it.

Audubon Guide to Attracting Birds, edited by John H. Baker (Doubleday). Contains more about activities with birds than its name implies.

Wildlife and Plants by A. C. Martin, H. S. Zim, and A. L. Nelson (Whittlesey House). Comprehensive data on food and feeding habits of many American waterfowl, songbirds, and gamebirds.

INDEX

Asterisks (*) denote pages on which birds are illustrated

RECORDS

RECORDS